'If you've ever thought that belief in God cannot be squared with the existence of a natural world that teems with viruses, parasites, earthquakes, tsunami and a host of other horrible ways to kill us, then this compelling, informative and lucidly argued book will make you think again.'
Professor Nick Megoran, School of Geography, Politics and Sociology, Newcastle University, UK, and author of *Big Questions in an Age of Global Crises*

'I don't recommend this book for bedtime reading, for it raises profound and disturbing questions. But therein lies its greatest value. Sharon Dirckx offers no easy answers. In fact, she makes clear that we will never fully understand natural disasters this side of eternity. But her book compelled me to examine my shallow assumptions and dig down to bedrock truths about God, our broken world and our ultimate hope.'
Glenn Oeland, Senior Editor, *National Geographic*

'How can there be a good God when there are hurricanes, tsunami and starvation? This question is often overlooked in conversations around the problem of evil. Rather than shying away from disaster, disease and death, Sharon Dirckx demonstrates that Christianity has the resources to face these issues – as well as to give us hope in the midst of them.'
Lee Strobel, *New York Times* bestselling author and founding director, Lee Strobel Center, Colorado Christian University, USA

'The occurrence of disasters and all the associated grief and suffering that they cause poses a major problem for both religious and secular people. In a series of thoughtful chapters, Sharon Dirckx discusses how we might approach this problem, finally landing on a Christian perspective of hope even in the midst of perplexity. The chapters are interspersed with moving personal reflections from both survivors and

aid workers that keep the discussion grounded; they brought tears to my eyes.'
Bob White, FRS, Emeritus Professor of Geophysics, University of Cambridge, UK

'Using stories, science, Scripture and philosophy, Sharon helps us to think through the problem of suffering caused by natural disasters. This moving book is honest, and yet it is grounded in the hope of the Christian message.'
Clare Williams, founder of Get Real Apologetics

Dr Sharon Dirckx is a freelance speaker and author and an adjunct lecturer at OCCA, The Oxford Centre for Christian Apologetics. Originally from a scientific background, she has a PhD in brain imaging from the University of Cambridge and held research positions in the UK and USA before moving into the area of apologetics. Sharon speaks and lectures regularly and has appeared on several BBC programmes in the UK, including Radio 2's *Good Morning Sunday* and Radio 4's *Beyond Belief*. She is author of the award-winning book, *Why?: Looking at God, evil and personal suffering*, as well as *Am I Just My Brain?* Sharon lives in Oxford with her husband and two children.

BROKEN PLANET

BROKEN PLANET

If there's a God, then why are there
natural disasters and diseases?

Sharon Dirckx

INTER-VARSITY PRESS
36 Causton Street, London SW1P 4ST, England
Email: ivp@ivpbooks.com
Website: www.ivpbooks.com

First published 2023

British Library Cataloguing-in-Publication Data
A catalogue record for this book is available from the British Library.

ISBN: 978–1–78974–092–9
eBook ISBN: 978–1–78974–093–6

Set in 11.75/15.5pt Minion Pro
Typeset in Great Britain by CRB Associates, Potterhanworth, Lincolnshire
Printed in Great Britain by Ashford Colour Press Ltd, Gosport, Hampshire

Produced on paper from sustainable sources

*Inter-Varsity Press publishes Christian books that are true to the Bible and that
communicate the gospel, develop discipleship and strengthen the church for its
mission in the world.*

*IVP originated within the Inter-Varsity Fellowship, now the Universities and
Colleges Christian Fellowship, a student movement connecting Christian Unions
in universities and colleges throughout Great Britain, and a member movement
of the International Fellowship of Evangelical Students. Website: www.uccf.org.uk.
That historic association is maintained, and all senior IVP staff and committee
members subscribe to the UCCF Basis of Faith.*

For Abby and Ethan

Contents

Acknowledgments

Broken Planet has come into being with the help of many people. I am grateful to my agent, Mark Sweeney, and to IVP for publishing this book, and especially to my former and current editors, Eleanor Trotter and Joshua Wells respectively. A book of this kind, seeking to draw from experiences of natural disasters from around the world, would not have been possible without the help of the international network that I was part of during its inception. A huge thank you to OCCA The Oxford Centre for Christian Apologetics for helping to identify people with a story to tell. Tracy Trinita, thank you for sitting me down and sharing your heart for a book of this kind. I am grateful to Nancy Gifford for support and vision in getting the project started back in 2019 and to Richard Giles for some key introductions in 2021. I am especially indebted to Kate Faccini, for help in setting up each interview, for your insights as a geographer and for your careful transcription of each interview. This book simply wouldn't have happened without you! The manuscript is all the better for insightful comments from friends and skilful apologists: Lara Buchanan, Tom Price, Max Baker Hytch, Simon Edwards and Nick Megoran. As for my family, your patience, understanding and encouragement gave me the freedom to write on the many evenings, weekends and school holidays that were needed. Heartfelt thanks to my husband, Conrad, for your unwavering support and crucial comments that are a litmus test for me of whether or not my writing 'will fly', and to my children, Abby and Ethan, to whom this book is dedicated.

Acknowledgments

Final thanks go to those who have shared their stories, not all of whom were able to feature in the final version of this book. You are the true heroes of this project and have reminded us what it means to live with courage, love your neighbour and serve God.

Tsunami, Sri Lanka 2004: morning

Rosi, tourist

We were on holiday and just finishing breakfast when somebody looked out of the window and commented that the sea was doing something rather strange. People started gathering to look for themselves. The sea was unusually high and seemed to be coming in closer. At first it was just a curious sight and we went over to watch as well.

All of a sudden, the sea was coming up the beach, over a wall and across the grass, and began to surround our building. Then the water level seemed to be rising. I registered how fast this was happening when I saw a lamp post knocked over directly under the restaurant. At that point, the atmosphere moved from one of curiosity to one of urgency and panic. We had no idea what was happening.

We were urged to move up some external stairs that led to the roof and so we picked up the children and swiftly made our way upwards along with some of the other guests. We stood at the top of the staircase and watched as the water rose to the level of the restaurant and ripped off parts of the balcony. All I could think of was the children. How can we hold on to them and save them? What will we do if the water gets any higher?

At this point, I prayed out loud to Jesus, asking him to save us. I tried to think about Jesus calming the storm, but this storm somehow felt too big. It was terrifying. I like to think my prayer was said in faith, but it was a desperate cry. I was really, really frightened, and couldn't imagine God intervening.

Then the water stopped rising and started to recede. At its peak, the water had reached to where we had been eating breakfast. As we looked out, we saw muddy water everywhere. You could not make out the swimming pool from the sea. People were clinging on to palm trees for their lives. The beach where our children had played happily the day before was now an empty shell. The sea had receded, exposing the whole bay as a barren crater. We didn't know that we had only twenty minutes before the second wave would hit.

There was a sense of urgency to get to higher ground. We moved as fast as we could, following whoever was in front, and wading past boats, fire extinguishers and other debris. No-one was talking.

When we got to the main road, it was total chaos. Everything seemed upside down. A car was standing upright on its nose. I saw a woman being carried towards us and felt sick with fear. We didn't feel nearly high or safe enough and began to panic. A Sri Lankan man appeared and showed us a track into the bushes which went uphill. I remember thinking, this is what it feels like to be running for my life and the lives of my children.

We eventually reached a clearing, where there were a couple of houses. The owners were amazing, serving bananas, tea and even curry later on in the day. Most of the people from the hotel congregated there and gradually more villagers started to arrive. Everyone was in shock and mobile phones were being passed around as people tried to make contact with the outside world. Slowly the bigger picture started to emerge.

Those who returned to the hotel came back with stories of mass looting in the time between waves. Many villagers had lost

10

loved ones. I met a lady who had two boys at her side. One of them, about ten years old, had played with my daughter on the beach. Just two days earlier, he had seemed a cheeky little boy, full of life, but now he was drenched and confused. I hardly recognized him. The woman gestured to me that she had lost a third child. I hugged her and cried with her and prayed for her. There were repeated screams of grief from one of the houses. Other people cried silently. Many did not know if their families were OK.

We were in a remote corner of Sri Lanka, with just the clothes on our back and no idea of the full scale of the disaster. I did have a sense that rescue would come, but there was absolutely nothing we could do to speed this up. We were totally dependent on the kindness of those around us, and of course God.

Introduction

On 26 December 2004 millions watched their TV screens in disbelief as a wall of water surged onto beaches in Thailand, Indonesia and southern India, destroying homes, entire families and livelihoods. Up to 230,000 people were killed and 1.74 million displaced, and many thousands were injured or missing. In 2005, Hurricane Katrina decimated parts of New Orleans, and many other cities and neighbourhoods in Mississippi, Alabama and Florida, leaving as many as 1,833 dead[1] and more than a million displaced in the Gulf Coast region.[2] We could also call to mind the Japan 2011 earthquake and tsunami, the devastation in Haiti in 2010, and the havoc wreaked across the Caribbean in 2018.

It is impossible to go more than a couple of months without hearing of a new disaster of some kind. And yet a large-scale natural disaster of another kind has also swept across the globe in recent years. At the time of writing, the coronavirus has infected almost 580 million people and has claimed nearly 6.5 million lives. During March and April 2020, up to a third of the world's population was in lockdown, with huge implications for households, families and communities, not to mention educational and economic spheres. We have all been brought face to face with the global pandemic caused by the COVID-19 virus.

How do we make sense of natural disasters? One of the strongest objections to the Christian faith is the question of suffering. Suffering is one of the biggest barriers to belief in God. When Christians respond, a key part of their argument is to give what is known as a free will defence and highlight that humans can make choices for ill that can bring about suffering in the lives of others. Yet, a free will defence is helpful only in accounting for what philosophers call *moral evil* – evil relating to how humans behave. A very different kind of response is needed to make sense of *natural evil* – evil that impacts the natural world itself, either through geophysics in the case of natural disasters, or through our biology in the case of disease and sickness.

Questions about natural disasters are expressed in many ways. The premise behind each question is that events such as earthquakes, tsunami and pandemics seem to happen *regardless* of our choices, not because of them. Even if people are responsible for their actions, we are surely not responsible for natural disasters? They are caused by forces much bigger than us. Our insurance policies protect us against 'Acts of God'. If God exists, then why does he let them happen? Is the profound suffering and loss caused by natural disasters yet more evidence that God does not exist? (I will refer to God as 'he' throughout this book because the Bible consistently uses the male pronoun. This is not to infer that God is male, but rather that he is a person rather than an 'it'.)

Broken Planet will take a closer look at some of the questions that we ask about natural disasters. But answers and arguments that appeal to the intellect will only get us so far. We also need to hear from those with first-hand experience of earthquakes, tsunami, hurricanes, flooding, wildfires, drought, locust infestations and pandemics, as well as from those who have experienced war, famine and refugee crises. You will hear stories from around the world, those of humanitarian aid workers, chaplains, doctors, tourists and local residents. Each person was interviewed and the words you will read are their own. Some were working for NGOs to bring emergency relief in the aftermath of a disaster. Others survived the disaster itself, which yields a suffering of its own: not just flashbacks of their trauma, but also survivor's guilt – why they survived when so many others didn't. These stories are not simply a supplement to make the book as a whole more readable. They are arguments *in themselves* and are intended as 'stand-alone' narratives that weave among the chapters dealing with philosophy and science.

In the process of taking the interviews, I was shocked to repeatedly hear that this was the first time anyone had ever asked about their experiences, and of how hard it can be to relay the trauma they have seen on the front lines of life's worst situations to friends and family back home. For some, their stories have never been told before, and so I count it a privilege to have been able to sit with each person and listen. Some said that if their story could help someone else, then it was a story worth sharing. For this reason alone, this book will have been worth it.

We are not going to be able to 'bottom out' every question on natural disasters; how could we possibly hope to on such a vast subject! You will notice that each person featured in the book has a lived experience of faith in God and shares his or her story from this point of view. You may not share those beliefs, but my hope is that you will be able to take their perspectives on board as you think through your own questions. Even though there is much we don't understand, each person would say that they had seen God, whom they call Jesus, at work in very real ways, even amid widespread catastrophe.

Tsunami, Indonesia 2004

John, paediatrician

We flew into Medan ten days after the tsunami. The local government said that they were going to send us to a village called Lhoong that had had no medical relief. We took an overnight bus to the city of Banda Aceh and the scene on arriving was horrific. You've seen the photos. Ships on the streets. Debris and mud everywhere. People's homes and possessions had been stacked by the waves into huge piles that looked like giant sets of pick-up sticks. This was a heavily Islamic area that was also experiencing political upheaval. Kidnappings were not uncommon, so we had to be careful.

It took just twenty minutes to make the 35-mile trip from Banda Aceh to Lhoong. As the helicopter followed the coastline, we took in the scenes below us. We should have been looking at fishing villages. Instead, we saw places where villages used to be. The concrete foundations were visible, the village footprint, but everything else had been swept clean. In the aftermath of an earthquake, which I have also experienced, you usually see piles of rubble close to the disaster, but here it was very different. Everything was gone. The rubble was 2 miles inland. Lhoong had been hit by not one but three successive 60-ft-high waves. It really was ground zero of the 26 December tsunami, and we were the first team to go in.

As soon as we stepped out of the helicopter, a relief worker ran up to me asking, 'Are you the paediatrician? Can you look at this sick kid?' They handed me a toddler who had a fever. My two colleagues, doctors in emergency medicine and family practice, were also immediately handed children to examine. Inside the child's mouth were Koplik spots, which are an early sign of measles, a highly contagious disease that could easily rip through a refugee camp. The child needed quarantining and we started giving vitamin A to everyone we could get to. Everyone was shell-shocked and we were still getting tremors from the initial earthquake.

We were sent to Lhoong because of its large refugee population, consisting of people from thirteen neighbouring villages. Lhoong is also home to a hospital that serves the region, but at this time it was completely overwhelmed. Many of its doctors were from further away, and when the tsunami hit, they returned home to help their own families. Acehnese rebels had also kidnapped one of the nurses to provide care for the rebels. So medical personnel were urgently needed on the ground.

Initially, we spent a lot of time treating injuries. We irrigated wounds, sutured lacerations and treated infections such as pneumonia. Unfortunately, we didn't have a tetanus vaccine, which would have been helpful. A lot of kids were having respiratory problems, similar to asthma, from having inhaled various things during the tsunami. So we made some makeshift inhalers out of plastic bottles.

We learned that, of the twelve thousand people living in the region, nearly half had perished. The closest fishing village down the hill was called Saney. Before the tsunami, Saney had seventy-three buildings and 270 residents. When we arrived, there were only seventy survivors, and no remaining buildings. Some of the boys we treated had survived by climbing trees, but even in the trees they still got hit by the enormous waves. We were told that not one family was left intact. One woman came to the hospital with a boy. Through our translators, we learned that she had lost her entire family. The boy was not a relative; he was the only surviving member of his family, so the woman had said to the boy, 'You're my son now,' and took him in as her own. There was a lot of beauty even in the midst of horrific loss.

We were a team of three doctors, four translators and one logistics coordinator, working with the relief agency Food for the Hungry (FFH). Most of us had flown in from China, but our logistics person was from the United States and one translator was from Kuala Lumpur. Just as crucial as any medical care was the role of our translators in sitting with the bereaved. Many of these families needed someone to process their experiences with, just to tell their story, but they couldn't speak to their neighbours because everyone was grieving. What they needed was someone from the outside to come in and just listen. So, while we were giving out medicine and making inhalers, some of our translators were sitting and giving their time and attention to the grief-stricken. We all entered into the suffering of those around us and carried the burden of their pain.

We should have included a female doctor on our team because many mothers and pregnant women refused to see a male doctor. But, on one occasion, I was allowed into the delivery room to examine a newborn having some difficulties. This experience took me back to my own story, as I was born near Beirut into a war zone and evacuated to the USA as a six-month-old baby. With my limited Arabic, I was at least able to greet this family and explain to them through the translator that my father's name was Salim, which means 'peace'. The baby's father, moved by my story, decided that Salim would also be the name of their little boy.

The people were incredible. They welcomed us, they fed us like you wouldn't believe, and they gave us the best coffee I've ever had in my life. And we were running on caffeine and not sleeping much. Every so often, I would just break down in tears, take a moment, and then go back to work.

Each afternoon, the village shut down while everyone took a nap. One afternoon, the family practice doctor and I started playing soccer with the local kids. Over the years, I've thought a lot about how best to help children who are stuck in refugee camps and natural disasters. My conclusions? Kids just need to play. That soccer game was great fun for everyone and therapeutic for the children.

I didn't come across many locals asking why the tsunami had happened to them. I wonder if part of the reason was that, even without natural disasters, life is hard for these Indonesian villagers. Suffering is a part of daily experience. Poverty, disease and death are never far away, and when a series of 60-ft waves hits, people are not surprised.

The only time I came across someone asking 'why?' was among relief workers. Back in Medan, each different country bringing relief would set up a tent topped with its national flag. There were contingencies from across the world, except that the wealthy Arab Gulf countries were distinctly absent. Why would Saudi Arabia and UAE neglect to help the most populous

Muslim country in the world? A relief worker from the Red Crescent, who was not a Muslim, provided the answer. 'The Muslim countries aren't giving because they feel like this is God's judgment. If [the Indonesians] were good Muslims, and if their worship was better, this would not have happened.'

Working in medicine has forced me to engage with suffering. I have had many children die right in front of my eyes, in a fully equipped paediatric intensive care unit in the USA as well as on a dirt-floor shack in a Chinese slum. The pain, suffering, loss and death in Lhoong were the same, only on a massive scale, but the goal was always to engage, serve, and help bear the burden of pain. The question 'why?' was to be wrestled with later.

The day we left was a Muslim holiday, and the USA were not flying any helicopters that day. If we could just get back to Banda Aceh the remaining legs of the journey would line up and we'd be home within a couple of days. The biggest challenge was getting back up the coast to Aceh. Our translator from Kuala Lumpur, in a somewhat pejorative and sassy tone, said, 'Well, why don't you guys pray? Every time you pray God answers you.' So we did. 'God, we'd like to get back to our families, we'd like to get back home – can you provide a way?' We said 'Amen', and two minutes later we heard the whirring of rotary blades. Two Australian helicopters had landed. They could take us back to Banda Aceh and had the exact number of spare seats on board to bring each member of our team. The girl from Kuala Lumpur shook her head, saying, 'This is just amazing.' Shortly after her return home, she came to faith in Jesus Christ.

To celebrate the Muslim holiday that day, the whole village paraded through the streets. All the women were dressed in white. It was beautiful and must have been healing for the village to continue with their traditions even in the midst of suffering and loss. It was as though they were saying together, 'We will continue on.'

1

If God is real, why are there natural disasters?

I can remember the moment when news of the 2004 tsunami came in. For many, the day after Christmas is the time to finally relax after the furore of activity. Seated in a comfortable chair with a full stomach and family close by, we watched scenes of devastation unfold in the Indian Ocean. The contrast could not have been starker.

In the early morning, an earthquake measuring 9.0 on the Richter scale tore through the ocean bed near Banda Aceh in northern Indonesia triggering a huge surge of water along the Sumatran coastline reaching as far as Somalia. There was barely a few minutes' warning of the impending deluge. This was the deadliest tsunami since records began.

The impact of natural disasters is hard to comprehend, especially from an armchair in the seismically stable UK. News teams do their best to capture footage but, even then, the scale and intensity are hard to imagine. Eyewitness accounts such as those from Rosi and John bring us closer to the terror and trauma. One aid worker involved in the response to Meulaboh, Aceh Province, described there being

a line in the sand one kilometre in from the coast. Everything before the line has gone. Here and there the foundation stone of a building remains, but nothing more. Many of the thousands who perished here remain buried under tonnes of sand and mud washed in by the tsunami. It is a scene of total devastation. A photo of Hiroshima after the atom bomb came to mind.[1]

Natural disasters like these cause all kinds of questions to arise. If God exists, then why do they happen? Some argue that such widespread and needless suffering surely goes against the grain of belief in a God who claims to be good and have power over the forces of nature. In a matter of minutes, villages are swept away, families are wiped out, landscapes are obliterated as far as the eye can see, children are orphaned, mothers are left childless.

In the aftermath of the Indian Ocean tsunami, it took just two days for questions to surface in the mainstream media. On 28 December, an article entitled 'How Can Religious People Explain Something Like This?' was published in *The Guardian* expressing the sentiments of many:

A non-scientific belief system, especially one that is based on any kind of notion of a divine order, has some explaining to do . . . What God sanctions an earthquake? What God protects against it? Why does the quake strike these places and these peoples and not others? What kind of order is it that decrees that a person who went to sleep by the edge of the ocean on Christmas night should wake up the next morning engulfed by the waves, struggling for life?[2]

On the other side of the Atlantic, the heart of the problem was voiced in this way:

for those who believe in a God who has intervened in history . . . a God who can raise and lower the waters . . . has miracles at his disposal, and should be able to separate the sheep from the goats, the saints from the sinners: For that sort of God, the indiscriminate slaughter of 100,000 saints and sinners – children and parents alike – presents more of a problem. If God is responsible for the fall of a sparrow, it's hard to exempt him from other, more dramatic natural developments.[3]

How do we make sense of natural disasters? They seem to happen in spite of humans, not because of them. Many other large-scale disasters, such as the decimation at Hiroshima and Nagasaki in the Second World War, can be explained in terms of human action. But catastrophes such as earthquakes, tsunami, hurricanes, tornadoes and volcanic eruptions, to name a few, are different. The reality of suffering raises some of the hardest questions we can face and presents a huge barrier to faith in a loving God. Why any God would allow the seemingly indiscriminate devastation wrought by natural disasters is harder still.

What kind of God?

Actor and atheist Stephen Fry, in a 2015 feature on Irish national TV, was asked by interviewer Gay Byrne what he would say to God if it turned out to be true that God existed, and he found himself at the 'pearly gates'. Fry's response went viral and has since been viewed over 8 million times on YouTube:

It's known as theodicy, I think. I'll say, 'Bone cancer in children? What's that about? How dare you! How dare you create a world where there is such misery that is not our fault! It's not right. It is utterly, utterly evil. Why should I respect a capricious, mean-minded, stupid god who creates a world that is so full of injustice and pain? That's what I'd say.'[4]

Fry goes on to say more and, at its core, his objection is to the needless and preventable suffering of innocents due to forces beyond their control. It is an objection to another kind of natural evil. And who wouldn't agree with him? That any parent should have to bury and grieve a child goes against the natural order. These words may or may not capture the whole of Fry's beliefs and opinions on this matter, but nevertheless they capture the strength of emotion that questions of suffering can evoke in us, especially when we try to bring God into the conversation. Belief in a good and powerful God seems wholly inconsistent with the needless and horrendous suffering that many face, and the inconsistency becomes most acute when the suffering is severe. Fry is angry at the notion of this kind of God. He is not alone in his reaction.

In their mind's eye, many form a mental picture of some sort of God. If there is a God who allows such terrible natural disasters, they imagine this God must be sadistic, uninterested or just weak. Perhaps these traumatic events are simply divine mood swings? Discussions on the problem of evil are not new – people have wrestled with this question for millennia. The writings of ancient Greek philosopher Epicurus, as summarized by eighteenth-century philosopher and atheist

David Hume, put it like this: 'Is [God] willing to prevent evil, but not able? Then he is impotent. Is he able but not willing? Then he is malevolent. Is he both able and willing? Whence then is evil?'[5]

This particular challenge is central to Judeo-Christian belief because it speaks of a God who is *love* yet is also *powerful* and in ultimate control over the events of history and the forces of nature. In contrast, all other belief systems do not hold together these two facets in quite the same way. Consider polytheism, the belief in many gods, characteristic of the ancient Greek and Roman worlds and some forms of Hinduism today. Each god has limited control over a particular force of nature, and can act with kindness or caprice, as the mood takes him or her. There is no compulsion to act with love, nor does any one deity have ultimate control. Or we could consider Islam, in which Allah is sovereign over all but able to bring about both good and evil. In this case, power is central, but not necessarily the obligation to act in love. Or we could look at some forms of Buddhism that strive not towards love as such, but towards detachment from the categories of this world, into a state of pure existence. Again, love and power are not held in tension in quite the same way.

The Christian idea of God points to a completely loving and powerful God and therefore needs to make sense of suffering in the light of this. When it comes to moral evil, evil stemming from how people behave, Christians often point to a *free will defence*.[6] We live in a world in which humans have been given by God the dignity of freedom to live and behave as they wish, rather than be controlled as puppets or automatons. Yet, as a result, they are capable of bringing about good *and evil* in the lives of others. In other words, a good deal of suffering is caused by humans, one to another. The free will defence is central to making sense of moral evil, but a different kind of answer is needed when making sense of natural evil. So, we keep returning to the question: why would a loving God allow natural disasters that sweep people away in a moment?

Just the way the world *is*?

To begin to think through this question, it's worth thinking about our options for making sense of natural disasters if God does *not* exist. If God does not exist, the universe is a closed system of matter that operates according to established laws of nature. This is just the way the world is. Scientists appeal to explanations such as cause and effect, probability and adaptation.

One explanation is that disasters happen because one physical event leads to another according to the laws of nature. Chains of events are set in motion by a particular trigger. Cause and effect. In terms of tsunami and earthquakes, the earth's crust is segmented into tectonic plates (which we will say more about in chapter 2) that sometimes collide with one another, releasing shock waves on land and at sea. The laws of nature follow fixed patterns.

Second, scientists could also look to probabilistic explanations. There are thought to be on average 500,000 earthquakes every year, but only 100,000 of them are strong enough to be felt and only 100 cause damage.[7] In other words, 0.02% of all earthquakes lead to human suffering. These are fairly good odds considering the earth is moving beneath our feet, but with half a million occurrences per year, by chance alone every so often there will be a big one.

Third, scientists might appeal to evolutionary explanations. It's pointless trying to find deeper reasons for why some survived whereas others didn't. Perhaps some people were slightly better adapted to their environment and able to run faster to higher ground or climb and hang onto a nearby tree with greater strength. Others were simply in the wrong place at the wrong time. Martin Kettle, writing in *The Guardian*, argued that the 'scientific belief system' leaves no room for speculating as to why some survived and others didn't. After all, 'a mindless natural event' is indiscriminate in its destruction.[8] Earthquakes and tsunami are merely outworkings of the forces of nature.

Though scientific descriptions may be factually correct, we still do find ourselves asking deeper questions. We find ourselves asking 'Why me?', 'Why them?', 'Why now?' and 'Does my suffering matter?' If we look just to the sciences to make sense of natural disasters, we can end up emotionally void.

To call an event a 'disaster' is to make a moral judgment, to imply that something is *wrong*, that things could or should be better than they are. Yet, scientific accounts alone can't take us to this destination. The sciences merely tell us how things are, not how they *should be*. They describe events in the natural world with elegance and insight but are under no obligation to infer that nature *ought* to be a certain way. Why then do we insist that they should? We *Homo sapiens* seem to have an intrinsic awareness of right and wrong. Regardless of what our particular beliefs might be, we are unavoidably moral beings. People express their morality in different ways.

Altruism

A recent article in *Time* magazine, entitled 'Want to Do More Good?',[9] unpacks how many in the West want to live today not just with their own interests in mind, but also for the 'greater good'. This movement, known as Effective Altruism (EA), is partly driven by environmental concerns, and recognizes that our choices today, even in relatively mundane matters, could have a huge effect on people in other parts of the world and on countless millions in the future. Finding ways to help others is an important part of what it means to live responsibly, in order that 'humanity might [not] permanently derail its future', and is also life-giving and liberating. EA advocates live according to a morality that 'value[s] all lives equally and act[s] on that basis'. Ethicist Peter Singer is a vocal advocate of the EA movement, having established a charity that helps people identify effective ways in which they can help others. He described its aim in a 2017 TED Talk as 'How to do the most good to make the world a better place'.[10]

We will discuss the practical edge of Effective Altruism in more detail in chapter 10, when we consider what our response might be to natural disasters. Singer and others have certainly mobilized many into living for the good of others, and have no doubt made the world a better place as a result. Altruistic approaches harness the selfless side of human nature; however, a cursory glance at the newspapers reminds us that there is also a darker side. People can be extraordinarily selfish and seek to live for the good of themselves, usually at the expense of others. Surely we need a moral framework that can make sense of both altruism and egotism? Of the human capacity to show extraordinary compassion but also unimaginable cruelty?

Furthermore, where does the belief that all lives are equally valuable ultimately come from? There have certainly been many cultures, empires and influential people across the centuries who have been unapologetic about their view that some humans are of greater value than others. For example, Greek philosopher Plato in his dialogue *Gorgias* said of human beings that 'justice consists in the superior ruling over and having more than the inferior'.[11] In other words, some people were simply *born* with greater worth than others; slavery in the ancient world rested on this very principle. Aristotle believed that 'the relation of male to female is by nature a relation of superior to inferior and ruler to ruled'.[12] It seems that the battle of the sexes has been going on for many centuries.

The belief that all people have inherent and equal value has not come from nowhere, even though it seems self-evident today. Historians such as Tom Holland make the point that human dignity has its roots in the biblical understanding that all people are made and loved by God.[13] The concept of human 'rights' emerged during the Middle Ages on precisely this basis.

Cultural morality

Another view is that morality is cultural, and that different traditions and tribes have their own accepted moral values. But if that is so, why are there worldwide campaigns to abolish the trafficking of men, women and children, regardless of their cultural context? And why are there always people who are not content to simply accept the values they are being fed, especially when those values lead to oppression and abuse?

A friend of mine was born and raised in poverty in a Ugandan slum into a culture in which the abuse, rape and prostitution of children is culturally normal. This friend has dozens of girls in her care who have been harmed or are at risk of abuse, whom she has made it her vocation to help. I heard recently of a child who was made to sleep with an older relative for eating a piece of chicken that had been reserved for her mother. Poverty is a dehumanizer. Yet the response of the child was not simply to accept the societal norm. Instead, she ran to my friend's house, to safety. Not all societal practices are so extreme. Some are more benign. But the extremes are needed to show that a cultural basis for morality is insufficient. Resistance to the values of the culture suggests that there is a framework for morality that sits beyond culture.

We also know that whole countries and continents have overturned deeply held cultural values in favour of better ones. Look no further than the transatlantic slave trade that was considered culturally acceptable in the Western world between the sixteenth and nineteenth centuries, but is viewed by most as abhorrent today. Such a cultural shift is possible only if there are moral standards that lie beyond the practices and norms of a particular society. Human awareness of right and wrong seems to be universal in its scope, transcending traditions, cultures and historical context. For this reason, attempts to explain morality in terms of societal values ultimately fail.

Objective morality

A growing number of philosophers today, known as non-theistic moral realists, believe that objective moral values do exist, but that God is not needed to explain them. Moral realists agree with Christians that we cannot truly make sense of humanity without reference to objective standards of right and wrong. Traditionally, Christians have argued that object-ive morality is grounded only in God. Moral realists, on the other hand, believe that there are certain 'basic ethical facts' in this universe that don't originate from any external source. They simply exist. As philosopher Erik Wielenberg put it,

> To ask of such facts, 'where do they come from?' or 'on what foundation do they rest?' is misguided in much the same way that, according to many theists, it is mis-guided to ask of God, 'where does He come from?' or 'on what foundation does He rest'? The answer is the same in both cases: They come from nowhere, and nothing external to themselves grounds their existence; rather, they are fundamental features of the universe that ground other truths.[14]

Non-theistic moral realism is a breath of fresh air and has directed philosophers to new ways of thinking about object-ive morality. As this shift away from relativism filters into everyday life, surely good will result. Yet, as we look more closely, questions arise. William Lane Craig and J. P. Moreland question what it means that moral values *just exist*?[15] They seem to exist in relation to people rather than as disconnected abstractions. William Wainwright takes this further in arguing that objective morality is not self-evident – it does require an explanation.[16] Where then do the best explanations lie? Those with no belief in God are of course just as capable of acting morally as those who do believe, but the important question here is, what kind of universe makes best sense of why we find ourselves here as morally sentient beings? In a godless and non-moral physical universe, human morality is certainly possible, but it would be an anomaly and somewhat unexpected. However, if God exists, then moral beings are to be entirely expected because moral values have been a foundational aspect of the universe right from the beginning. Therefore, we could say that the material world has been brought into being by a good God, but something has also gone wrong, giving rise to evil. Along these lines, objective moral values by which we judge things to be right or wrong make most sense *if* God exists.

For many, a world full of natural disasters is a world in which a God of love cannot possibly exist. Yet, it's actually if this God does exist that we find the most persuasive grounds for making sense of the hurt and pain in this world and that we experience in life. Our anger, frustration, sadness, grief and trauma are not things to be ignored, suppressed or glibly prayed away. They are justifiable and valid, and are pointers not away from God but towards him.

Earthquake, Haiti 2010

Dan, World Hope International, country director

At the time of the earthquake, I worked for the Wesleyan Church as area director for the Southern Caribbean. We were based on an island off the coast of Haiti called La Gonâve. When the earthquake began, it was quite obvious what was happening. Paintings and hangings began to fall off our walls, food slid from pantry shelves and furniture moved across the room. In a population of about 10 million, there were probably 3 million mobile phones, but coverage quickly went down for 90% of people. Radio and TV coverage in the local area was also down. We had a satellite phone and Internet and through these began to hear stories, receive calls and gradually piece together what had happened on the mainland. A friend called from Port-au-Prince. He was sobbing, and you must understand that this guy is a scientist. He's very controlled and not prone to emotion:

'It's all gone. It's destroyed.'

He had narrowly escaped with his life, having jumped out of a third-storey window onto the roof of a neighbouring building as the building he was in was collapsing. That call was my personal wake-up.

Being the tropics, it was dark by 6 pm, just an hour and a quarter after the earthquake had happened. I was out in the garden, on the station, and began to hear what Haitians call the *rèl*, an anguished cry that communicates to the community that a loved one has died. Near a hospital, you're likely to hear the *rèl* fairly frequently, and in neighbourhoods this cry is raised as a way of announcing a death. I began to hear the sound of this cry from all around me, from every direction, for hours. Only then did I begin to understand the scope of what had happened.

One of my wife's dear friends, Madam Felicienne, had worked for the mission as a cook for the previous twenty-five years. Her three children were good friends with our two girls. They were all bright young adults with strong Christian beliefs. They had been playing games and eating together on the Sunday evening because it had been the end of the Christmas break. The next morning, Monday, Madam Felicienne's children left the island, taking the public boat back to Port-au-Prince. On Tuesday the earthquake struck.

When there had been no news for twenty-four hours, a team of people was sent to their apartment in Port-au-Prince, only to find a pile of rubble on the ground. They began to ask questions and found out that the youngest daughter, a very athletic girl, had almost made it out of the building. As she was going through the front door of the apartment building, a piece of concrete from the upper storeys fell on her, crushing her spine and lower body. She didn't die immediately. Neighbours who had survived were trying to get her out from under the concrete when she passed away. The other two children never made it out of the building, but the team was able to recover their bodies.

There were so many bodies starting to be stacked up on the streets, and since this was the tropics, they very quickly began to decompose. The Government provided front-end loaders that were used to scoop piles of bodies from the ground and into massive dump trucks, to take them to mass graves on the outskirts of the city. There was something very brutalizing about this, but the practical reality was that we now faced an extreme health hazard and had to survive. The stench was indescribable in the city and lingered for years from Port-au-Prince down to Léogâne. So many of the bodies were under buildings and could not easily be recovered, and some weren't recovered for the better part of a year. As each building was excavated, the community would experience everything all over again. The grief. The stench. Everything.

To put a loved one on a pile and watch it be scooped up by a front-end loader and know that it was going to be dumped in a trench was probably one of the most traumatic things a Haitian could experience. Haitians have a lot of beliefs and customs related to death. Now we have an entire nation that has PTSD, partly because they haven't been able to grieve properly and go through the rituals of saying goodbye. The mass graves have been made into national memorials. I think that helps at some level, but it's still hard not knowing where loved ones are buried. Madam Felicienne knows where two of her children are buried. Her youngest daughter is an unknown because her body was placed at the curb and was taken away at an earlier time. This is just one of many, many stories.

The earthquake registered only 7 or 7.1 on the Richter scale, which wouldn't normally cause damage on this kind of scale. There may have been more going on with plate tectonics to make it so severe, but the biggest reason for this disaster was that the buildings were not built to withstand earthquakes. Concrete is the preferred building material, to mitigate against mildew, rot, termites, hurricanes and fire, but there's a tipping point beyond which it is no longer safe without steel support columns to add strength. A concrete building that's more than three or four storeys tall is very heavy and doesn't have any 'side-to-side' strength. A steel-reinforced building is able to move in an earthquake; a concrete building is not.

There are so many stories about buildings that were too tall and of corner-cutting in the quality of materials used. The only five-star hotel in Haiti at the time, The Montana, had seven storeys that pancaked into a pile. We also learned that the first big jolt from the earthquake shifted many buildings such that doors and windows could not be opened. I have seen hours of security footage from inside these buildings, showing people frantically running from door to door trying to open them. The footage ends with a cloud of dust.

Port-au-Prince filled up with emergency responders from all over the world within days, but other areas, such as Léogâne Petit-Goâve, were yet to be reached. About a week after the earthquake, our organization opened an emergency hospital in this area, close to the epicentre. One of our missionary staff was a medical doctor, and she was able to move down from the northern regions to help us. The Wesleyan Church had also previously established a hospital on the island of La Gonâve and was able to move staff and supplies from there to work in Léogâne Petit-Goâve. The US military gave us some tents and built a prefab building for us there.

For three months, my role was primarily to find medical supplies and to provide transportation for volunteer staff coming to and going from this emergency hospital. We were doing surgeries and delivering babies. Of primary importance was to treat and dress the hideous crush wounds that came from being trapped under a building for days or even weeks. One surgeon called it 'amputation hell', because he was having to remove limbs that would have been saved in another setting and not even been considered seriously injured. But many injuries were already quite septic by the time a doctor saw them.

Some team members were emotionally wrecked by their experiences and needed professional care. Most of us have lingering effects. I take medication every day and see my counsellor every week. I grew up in a 'skin your own skunks' kind of Appalachian culture where you don't ask for help, you only take it from people you trust. The construction world that I started out in is also a tough kind of environment, and so I had to do a bit of growing up to ask for and accept help. It was humbling to abruptly arrive at my limits and go past my capacity to cope, physically, mentally, emotionally and spiritually.

Every day is a disaster in Haiti. Things that you would use to qualify as a disaster are true in Haiti every single day. There is violence. The roads are some of the world's most dangerous. There is the Restavek system, a form of child slavery. There is hunger and people go without food every day. There is thirst because most of the population does not have access to clean water. There is disease. I've had malaria, dengue fever, Chikungunya and TB, all part of the risk of doing humanitarian work, but most local people have little access to health care. They just live or die. COVID has had little impact in Haiti, perhaps because significant comorbidity doesn't exist. People dying from COVID in Europe and the USA because of under-lying health conditions are already dead in Haiti.

From the night of the earthquake, churchyards became sanctuaries across the cities and countryside, safe places where people could expect to receive help and be cared for. Right from the beginning, people would be praying and singing, comforting one another and sharing their food and their blankets. Churches quickly became refuges for those with nowhere to go, and centres for the distribution of supplies. For six to eight months afterwards, the churches were seen as communities of protection. The church was doing exactly what the church should be doing at a time like this, involving all faith communities, be they Roman Catholic, episcopalian, Pentecostal, Baptist or indigenous local churches without a denominational affiliation. We also saw a very sig-nificant increase in church attendance that continued for years afterwards.

I think these faith communities were the single biggest reason why there has not been a significant mental health crisis in Haiti in subsequent years. In my opinion, there are two reasons for this. First, a spiritual framework is very protective when you're talking about post-traumatic stress because it allows a person to sort out and to make a sensible story out of what just happened. Even people of sincere faith have ques-tions. Where is God? What did God have to do with this? Why did so many people have to die? People with a spiritual frame-work seem to be better able to navigate these dilemmas than people without that spiritual framework. Second, the real and practical ways in which the church was able to serve needs was also remarkable and was made possible largely through local church connections.

Madam Felicienne was at work when the team returned from Port-au-Prince. In typical Haitian fashion, they wouldn't tell her anything until they were with her in person. I think she knew what that meant. Happy news would have been shared by phone. She reacted as you might expect. As I was holding this lady who is a dear friend of our family, a colleague, a woman of great character and absolute commitment to the work of the kingdom, I was struggling with the whole idea of sovereignty. It's one thing when sovereignty is an academic exercise or discussed in a theological conversation, but quite another when you are dealing with something like this, and asking, 'Really God, is this just, fair, loving?'

Part of the burden she bore was that she had insisted her kids go on Monday because they got a free boat ride back to the mainland. If they had waited until Wednesday, when they had wanted to go, they would have had to pay for the trip. But then they would not have been in that apartment at the time of the earthquake. That decision, or so she thinks even to this day, cost her children their lives. She was not in her rational mind for a period of weeks and it was heartbreaking to watch her grieve.

In humanitarian work, you must find that balance between deep caring for others and the ability to care for personal needs. You have to be able to find that centred place where you don't allow your heart to become a stone, but also maintain enough distance that you're able to function. After the things I saw and experienced, I managed to maintain my composure externally, but internally I was in spiritual crisis. Given the circumstances, that was not altogether surprising. Some of the things that privileged Christians believe to be true about God require a new understanding in a place like Haiti. You can go only so far with reasoning and intellect. There's always that next step that requires you to say, 'I believe.' Sometimes it takes a while to get there after a traumatic experience, because this process must go deeper than mental assent. But eventually I did get there.

2

Is this the best of all possible worlds?

Enlightenment thinker Gottfried Wilhelm Leibniz attempted to justify the ways of God to people by means of *théodicée*, or 'theodicy' in the English-speaking world. In his 1710 publication,[1] Leibniz argued that the world in which we find ourselves is indeed the best of all possible worlds and could not have been made by God any other way. The natural world has been arranged to enable the greatest possible good, and any resultant suffering is unavoidable. In short, 'All is well'.

Leibniz's thinking was considered sufficient for a time. That is, until the Lisbon earthquake of 1755. On the morning of 1 November, a series of earthquakes, the strongest being 9.0 magnitude, shook the Portuguese capital for a full ten minutes. Gaping holes several feet wide opened up in the streets. Buildings collapsed, crushing those inside. As it was a Sunday morning, and All Saints' Day, many were attending church, and even those who weren't planning to attend found themselves rushing inside for sanctuary from the hazardous streets. But that day, two-thirds of the city was reduced to rubble, including its historic churches and monuments. Many of those who survived the quake went on to drown in the 20-metre-high arc of water that inundated Lisbon's shores just half an hour later. Fires then broke out and burned for six days, taking yet more lives. In total, at least sixty thousand people perished, a quarter of the population of this previously prosperous and influential city.

After Lisbon, French philosopher Voltaire launched an attack on Leibniz's thinking through his 1759 novella and satire *Candide* and 1756 *Poème sur le désastre de Lisbonne*.[2] The 'best of all possible worlds' approach was deemed insufficient to deal with such extreme catastrophe.

'All is well,' you say, 'and all is necessary.'
Do you think this universe would be worse
Without the pit that swallowed Lisbon?
Are you certain that the great eternal cause,
The creator and knower of all things,
Could not have thrown us into this miserable world
Without forming volcanoes seething under our feet?
Do you set this limit for the supreme power?
Would you forbid him from exercising mercy?
Doesn't the eternal craftsman have
Infinite means available for his handiwork?

The question whether or not God could have made a better world is, of course, a matter of debate. There are philosophers who hold that this world is the best of all possible options, and there are those who believe it isn't – that God could have created a better world because ultimately there is no 'best-world scenario' that trumps all others.[3] Practically speaking, we only know the world that we have. Stories like Dan's from Haiti in 2010 leave us crying out for better worlds. Yet, as we think about other possibilities, we also need to 'zoom out' and take a closer look at conditions on Earth compared with our nearest neighbours, the other 'worlds' around us in the solar system.

It's a wonder life exists at all

The UK is well known for its variable weather. We take umbrellas everywhere, even in glorious sunshine, just in case it rains. I have even been known to take one to the desert while on holiday, much to the amusement of my hosts. Because of its variety, the British weather is a popular topic of conversation. We are quick to bemoan the conditions whatever they are, be it too wet, too dry, too hot, too cold, too sunny, too cloudy. And yet, when we consider the planets around us, our weather conditions and temperatures lie within such narrow limits that it is incredible that we exist at all.

For example, unmanned space missions to Venus reveal that its surface is covered almost entirely with volcanoes and volcanic lava plains, along with craters, and mountains.[4] Temperatures are high enough to melt lead. The 'air' consists of carbon dioxide and sulphuric acid, both of which are anathema to the human respiratory system. The atmosphere is so weighty that anything attempting to enter it would be crushed. One NASA report, in a beautifully understated manner, comments that 'the surface of Venus is not where you'd like to be'.[5] No human would survive a visit to this hostile planet.

If we move in the opposite direction, to Neptune and Jupiter, we see that they have storms that make ours look tiny by comparison – storms that call for a redefinition of the term 'extreme weather'. On Earth, the most powerful hurricane, a Category 5, may reach 215 mph (346 kph), yet on Jupiter, speeds may reach 384 mph (618 kph), almost double anything Earth can generate. Jupiter's 'Great Red Spot' is a storm larger than two of Earth's storms put together which has been gathering momentum and consuming smaller storms for more than four hundred years. It boasts freezing temperatures of around −163°C or −261°F. Life is as untenable on Jupiter as it is on Venus.

Recently, astronomers identified a new exo-planet, out-side our solar system, that rains liquid metal. Wasp-76b has local weather conditions that 'include 2,400°C temperatures, winds in excess of 10,000 mph and a steady pelting of iron rain'.[6] Something to call to mind the next time 'rain stops play' at Wimbledon or Lords. There are weather systems out there that are unimaginably hostile to living things. Conditions on Wasp-76b inspire awe and motivate artists and scientists alike to give their impressions of what it might look like. Yet none of us would come within a hair's breadth of living there.

To put it lightly, on all other planets in our solar system, and indeed every planet that we know of so far, life is untenable. The forces of nature render life inconceivable. And yet, here on Earth, although natural disasters do occur, they seem to be within boundaries such that life is still possible.

Natural causes

In the aftermath of the Lisbon earthquake, some were quick to attribute purely spiritual reasons for the disaster. However, natural philosopher Immanuel Kant sought to defuse this heated debate by pointing out that there are known natural causes behind earthquakes that help in our understanding of how and why they happen.[7] He was writing in the eighteenth century, and modern geophysics has seen to it that our understanding has developed further still today.

In the 1960s, geophysicists reached consensus, based on a publication from 1915,[8] that the earth's crust does not consist of one static and immobile shell, but a series of plates that are in motion. On Earth's surface are eight to twelve plates that fit together not unlike jigsaw pieces and move in different directions at different speeds in what is known as plate tectonics. Plate tectonics are known to be vital for life, as one article in *Scientific American* highlights:

> Our planet is in constant flux. Tectonic plates – the large slabs of rock that divide Earth's crust so that it looks like a cracked eggshell – jostle about in fits and starts that continuously reshape our planet – and possibly foster life . . . These plates ram into one another, building mountains. They slide apart, giving birth to new oceans that can grow for hundreds of millions of years. They skim past one another, triggering earth-shattering quakes. And they slip under one another in a process called subduction, sliding deep into the planet's innards and producing volcanoes that spew gases into the atmosphere. And not only is Earth alive, it is a vessel for life. Because it is the only known planet to host both plate tectonics – that ongoing shuffling of tectonic plates – and life, many scientists think the two might be related. In fact, some researchers argue that shifting plates, which have the ability to help regulate a planet's temperature over billions of years, are a crucial ingredient for life.[9]

Life and beauty

The same tectonics that cause earthquakes and tsunami are also crucial for fostering and sustaining life on earth. The process of subduction is a bit like taking a shovel to the ocean floor sediments. It carries carbon and other minerals essential to life deep beneath the continents, where they are heated up and melted, then erupted from volcanoes, enabling them to be recycled back into the biosphere.[10] Volcanoes also have a crucial role in bringing fresh nutrients and carbon dioxide from deep in the mantle beneath the earth's crust. Earthquakes are found mostly along the boundaries of the tectonic plates, where they relieve the stresses that are built up by the plate motions.

Eruptions also release back into the atmosphere nutrients and minerals that are crucial to life. Geophysicist Robert White argues that the importance of the carbon dioxide released back into the atmosphere cannot be understated. Without it, 'the planet would [likely] have been frozen for most of its history'.[11]

Furthermore, we know that the area surrounding a volcano is home to incredibly fertile soil beneficial in agriculture, which is partly why volcanic foothills became populated in the first place. I remember watching an Italian cookery programme on TV that featured a restaurant nestled in the crater of an extinct volcano. The fruit and vegetables served to guests were grown in the nearby mineral-rich volcanic soil and looked bigger and were tastier than anything that might have been harvested in more ordinary climes. Who can blame people for building towns and cities where the land is volcanically active? It seems there are also benefits.

Continental uplift is the reason why erosion, the gradual wearing-away of land, hasn't filled the oceans with silt and flattened the surface of the earth. There are mountain ranges that we climb up in the summer and ski down in the winter. All because of tectonic activity.

It would also be remiss not to mention that these same mechanisms create incredible natural beauty. I remember the first time I saw the Swiss Alps with my own eyes and being utterly speechless at picture-perfect splendour and majesty unlike anything I had seen before. Yet, an earth with no plate tectonics would be an earth with no Alps, Rockies, Dolomites or Himalayas. It would also be a world with no Hawaiian Islands, formed from cooled volcanic rock, and no Azores, which are actually the tip of mountain formations descending deep into the ocean. There would be no Lake District National Park in England with Scafell Pike to climb, nor the USA's Yellowstone National Park which attracts 4 million visitors a year. Some of Earth's most breathtaking habitats are formed through plate tectonics and volcanic activity. When we ask if this is the best of all possible worlds, are we asking for a world without stunning beauty?

In response, some may argue that even stunning beauty is a high price to pay for the devastation wreaked by streets rippling like carpets and bodies crushed beneath crumbling buildings. Perhaps many would happily trade a flat landscape for a world without earthquakes. At this point, geographers remind us that mountains themselves also play a vital role in the hydrological cycle, delivering water to rivers that provide vast areas with water. Warm air rises from the earth and as it encounters mountains it is forced to continue its journey upwards, until eventually it cools and falls on highlands as snow and rain. This precipitation then flows to lower lands in streams and then rivers, forming draining basins that enable millions of people to irrigate crops, feed cattle and drink water. Geophysicist Robert White points out that monsoons in the Himalayas provide water for 1,000 million people in India in this way.[12] Similarly, the Ethiopian mountains feed into the Nile River, and the Alps the Rhine. Mountain ranges are essential in enabling whole continents to teem with life.

Returning to the question of other 'worlds', we see that, however volatile Earth might seem through the lens of the frequent natural disasters we encounter, it is far more habitable than its neighbouring planets. Life is possible here, completely against the odds. More than that, the very mechanisms that trigger disasters such as earthquakes and tsunami also play a vital role in sustaining life on earth. Philosophers such as Richard Swinburne and Peter van Inwagen, along with the late theologian and physicist John Polkinghorne, make the case that natural disasters are the flip side of living in a world with stable natural laws that is able to sustain itself.[13]

Imagining other worlds

In conceiving of other possible worlds, we enter the mental gymnastics of trying to imagine a seismically stable planet that is able to sustain life. A planet that contains water but without plate tectonics, or one that has mineral-rich soil but with no volcanic activity to bring it from beneath the crust to the surface. Or a planet without locusts yet without unsettling whole ecosystems. Or bodies that can generate new cells but with no risk of cancers. We certainly can't rule out that God could have created different worlds with different laws, and as

Peter van Inwagen points out, our inability to conceive of such worlds does not mean they are impossible.[14] We must also take seriously Voltaire's charge that God could, in theory, have created a life-permitting universe without natural disasters, but has not done so. Given that he has not, does that bring his claims to power and goodness under the spotlight?

At this juncture, further questions arise. Does omnipotence mean having power to do absolutely anything? Surely if God is who he claims to be, there ought to be no bounds to his abilities? But can God create square circles? Can he make water in which it is impossible to drown? Can he create free beings who obey him at every moment? Can he create the law of gravity but also cause each person to hover just above the ground? Logically speaking there are actually many things that God cannot do, but this need not lead us to question his power. Rather, as particular laws of nature are set in place, certain outcomes automatically become more likely. In other words, the creation of a planet capable of sustaining itself brought with it the hazards of plate tectonics and volcanic eruptions. We simply couldn't have one without the other.

A 'perfect' or 'good' world?

As for whether this is the best of all possible worlds, the opening chapters of the Bible are helpful. Christians take a variety of positions on how long ago and by what process the events of Genesis 1 occurred, and much time has been spent on this emotive topic. My point here is to draw attention to the *kind of world* these verses describe. Five times during the creative process the same phrase is repeated: 'God saw that it was good.' The world we inhabit has been made *good*. Very good, in fact, after the arrival of *Homo sapiens*. But note, this is not the same thing as *perfect*. Perhaps there is a hint even here of the complexity of the natural world. It may or may not be the best of all possible options, and it certainly isn't perfect. But it is good. And sufficiently good that God himself was prepared to walk its streets.

The fact that we live on a life-permitting planet can also be seen as an expression of God's love and goodness. Complex sentient beings exist in a habitat of extraordinary diversity and life. And we do so despite the incredibly hostile conditions on every other planet and beyond the 2 miles vertically above and below us. Human existence is so incredibly unlikely, and yet here we are.

Philosophers such as Stephen Wykstra make a case that God may have reasons for permitting the particular world we find ourselves in, even if those reasons are not obvious or intuitive to us.[15] But are those reasons enough to make it worth the scale of suffering caused? Perhaps it would have been better not to exist at all? As we remember the story of Madam Felicienne and countless Haitians like her, we must feel the full force of this question. Of course, now we are into the realm of possibilities that time-limited people are simply not able to assess. The reality is that we exist, and since that is all that we know, how can we possibly comment on non-existence? The biggest loss of life in Haiti also seemed to be due not simply to the kind of world we live in, but also to the substandard buildings that people had constructed. We will discuss this more in chapter 3.

Those caught up in natural disasters have often found 'Why?' questions to be futile, and it can be more helpful to ask, 'What now?' Is there a way through this painful situation? Is there a way to face tomorrow? It seemed in Haiti that, as people carried one another's burdens and cared for one another, unbearable suffering somehow became bearable.

Hurricane Irene, USA 1999

Marjory, local resident

I grew up with hurricanes, as does anyone raised in my particular area of the States. I almost prefer hurricanes to earthquakes because hurricanes let you know that they're coming; earthquakes don't. Every July we would start getting ready. And you could see the differences from neighborhood to neighborhood. Wealthy households would put massive hurricane shutters over their windows. People would be taping up the windows, filling up jugs of water, gathering flashlights. Hordes of people would go to Costco to stock up on water, toilet paper and canned foods.

Our version of getting ready was always a bit different from other people's. The person of faith in my home was my mom and she would go from room to room praying Psalm 91, placing her hands on the walls and asking the Lord to protect us:

> Whoever dwells in the shelter of the Most High
>   will rest in the shadow of the Almighty.
> I will say of the LORD, 'He is my refuge and my fortress,
>   my God, in whom I trust.'
> (Ps. 91:1–2)

We repeated that psalm so much that I learned it by heart without even trying to memorize it. Early on in life, I remember finding safety in my mom's prayers. These were special words. They had power in them, and it was as though she was reciting something that came from heaven. Mom would also pray over me, which I found to be a little impractical, especially as I got older. I would look at my father who would be quite blasé about the approaching hurricane. I suppose that was because he had survived an earthquake. But you would have expected a scientist and doctor to take some serious precautions here. Yet throughout my childhood, that's how we got ready.

On 15 October 1999, Hurricane Irene, the sixth hurricane of the season, struck Florida. When we'd left the house to go to church earlier that day, it was just a regular Category 1 tropical storm, which everyone was accustomed to driving in. But on the way home, two hours later, things had taken a drastic turn into a hurricane Category 3, with winds going in both directions.

I'd insisted that we not go to church. But my mother was determined and the hurricane wasn't going to stop her. I was quite angry, to be honest with you. As a child, I desperately loved the Lord, but when I was a pre-teen my father left, my sister was diagnosed with schizophrenia and we had to move to a much smaller house. Questions like 'Why does God allow natural disasters?' are so loaded because the way you experience a natural disaster really depends on your other life experiences. It's not just about the hurricanes. They became much more scary after my father left.

I was angry. Angry that my sister was sick. Angry that my father had left. Angry that my mom was cleaning houses. I remember thinking that my mother's God didn't seem to be working for her. Sometimes my mom's prayers were a source of comfort to me, but sometimes they were a huge source of resentment because, I would ask, 'If you can listen to her prayers for the hurricane, why can't you listen to all the other prayers?' So I had begun to look to other religions because this one was clearly not working out. By then I was pretty deep into Islam.

That Sunday, my mom was just trying to get us home as quickly as possible. We couldn't take the streets, because the small roads flood easily in Miami, and the water can easily reach the level of the windshield on a car. We had to get to the freeway. I think we were driving a 1986 Oldsmobile, one of those four-door classic cars. These cars are actually quite scary because they are made of iron and don't fall apart upon impact. Instead, the passengers bear the force of any crash, so they're not very safe. Add to this that Miami is known for people with road rage. People will easily drive at 80 mph when the limit is 65, and police officers won't pull them over.

As we were driving home, the car behind rammed us, sending me flying towards the windshield. I was wearing a seatbelt but was so skinny and small that I would have gone right through it. My mom stuck out her hand, sending me flying back into the seat, and yelled out, 'The blood of Christ has power!' But I was thinking, my mom's Jesus isn't anywhere to be found and we're going to die. I thought it was crazy that she was calling down the power of heaven to protect us when it was very clearly the power of heaven sending this hurricane. But she didn't scream or lose her cool, and so I didn't either. I was really grateful for the self-control she had in that moment of danger.

We were in the middle lane and mom just calmly started to get over to the emergency lane at the roadside. We pulled over and got out. It was dark. Cars were whizzing by and at that point, a burning sensation came into my neck. I was in a lot of pain from whiplash. Someone pulled over to ask us if we were OK, and it only later dawned on us that that was the car that had reared us. We just wanted to get home, and so we got back into the car and somehow made it home before the full force of the hurricane landed. For Irene, we didn't have time to get ready in the usual way. It was just water, flashlights and the Psalms.

The eye of a hurricane is really peaceful because everything is moving around it. In that moment you're resting from the storm, but as the storm begins to move, then the rain begins to whiplash you like in a car wash. There's really no good position to be in, because the storm will keep moving no matter what. The hurricane itself isn't the most scary part. The problem is everything in its path that it sends flying. Like power lines. These would often collapse into flood waters, making the water 'live', and people would often die by being electrocuted as they tried to move through the water. It was the flooding and power lines that killed you. And the fires that started.

People also died from houses collapsing. As a kid, I became really good at predicting which houses were likely to survive and which would not. There's a neighborhood in Miami called Opa-locka, made up of mostly Haitian immigrants living in very small two-bedroom homes. These 'matchboxes' are built in an area that floods regularly, and they can easily collapse with the occupants still inside.

The neighborhood you lived in determined how you fared in a hurricane. In wealthy neighborhoods, a palm tree might go through someone's roof, but overall those homes were well prepared. Poorer neighborhoods had bigger issues that had very little to do with the hurricane itself. Not everyone had access to clean water. Buying in bulk requires a Costco membership, which costs money, and disposable income to stock up on extra things. But not everyone has enough money to do this. Credit cards might be another way. But a significant section of the population doesn't have access to credit, again affecting their capacity to 'stock up'.

Wealthier neighborhoods put sandbags around the houses and stacked them as a wall to keep the water out. But it was unreasonable to ask families with so little disposable income to spend hundreds of dollars on sandbags. There was a cheaper version in the form of mulch mixed in with rocks. People would do anything they could to keep the water away.

I've certainly cried, but mostly it's a cry of relief that comes from having survived. Before a hurricane, I would go room by room to pick out little things to take with me if we had to run away. The only thing that I ever picked up was a photo album. All I wanted to have with me were these particular pictures; everything else could go. I remember my mom having my sister's documents, my documents and hers – and that was it. That was all we needed. We held possessions lightly. For us, one of the biggest challenges was keeping my sister safe.

The year my dad left should have been the year my mom stopped being a Christian. If she had given up it would've made me feel better because then I would have been able to say that she was just a cultural Christian, and turn my back on it all as well. But my mom was like a pebble in my shoe because she just wouldn't stop believing. I had such respect for her and her prayers. They gave me pause, and that pause was enough to shake me into not dismissing it.

I remember being deeply frightened that it might be true. Not a childlike fear, such as when kids are afraid of what's in the closet or underneath the bed. Nor was it similar to when I'm afraid of a natural disaster. No, it almost felt like a fear that comes when you're confronted by truth. The fear of possibly one day coming face to face with God. As I grew older and I kept investigating the claims of my mother's faith, that feeling of fear always remained.

It actually took a really, really, really long time. I guess it was when I stopped feeling the fear and acknowledged 'Oh, this is true' that the fear turned into joy, and I finally surrendered. I would love to say that it was very easy for me, but it wasn't. In *Surprised by Joy*, C. S. Lewis says that he basically got dragged into the kingdom kicking and screaming. That's kind of it. I didn't expect it, but I've been surprised by Joy.

3

Why do *so many* suffer and die in natural disasters?

In 2005, a tropical storm with wind speeds of up to 175 mph ripped through the southern USA, decimating parts of New Orleans and many other cities and neighbourhoods in Mississippi, Alabama and Florida. Hurricane Katrina, which left 1,833 dead and 600,000 displaced, is remembered as one of the worst hurricanes to hit the USA in recent history.

The Caribbean islands are frequently devastated by hurricanes. Inhabitants and emergency services barely have time to regroup before the next storm hits. One of their most recent nemeses, Hurricane Dorian (2019), was one of the strongest Atlantic storms ever to make landfall.[1] Winds of up to 185 mph dispensed almost 1 metre of rainfall in the space of two days. Up to thirteen thousand homes were demolished in surge waters, and over seventy people killed, with many more missing.

Tropical storms, known as hurricanes, cyclones or typhoons depending on where they occur in the world, are huge spiralling storms that are drawn to areas with warm surface water. The Bay of Bengal, stretching from southern India through Bangladesh and Myanmar to Malaysia, suffers the most deadly storms in the world. In 1970, the Bhola cyclone struck shore, bringing severe flooding and storm surges of over 10 metres, and razing entire villages. An estimated half a million people died. We could also think of the 1999 super cyclone that claimed at least ten thousand lives in Orissa (Odisha), India, or Cyclone Nargis that wiped out 140,000 and displaced 2 million in the Irrawaddy Delta, Myanmar, in 2008. It is hard to capture in words 'the untrammelled fury of a super cyclone in the Bay of Bengal',[2] as one journalist put it.

A feature that often sets natural disasters apart from other types of suffering is the *scale* of suffering. When whole villages are washed away and many thousands are killed or displaced, the magnitude of loss is multiplied many times over. Why is it that *so many* people die in natural disasters? Philosophers such as William Rowe[3] and Paul Draper[4] refer to this as the evidential argument or problem of gratuitous evil. Why on earth would God allow such seemingly pointless evil on such a vast scale?

It is here that we begin to see that there is no such thing as a purely 'natural' disaster. Yes, there are natural factors; the forces of nature do what they do, and we have no control over them. But there are also human factors; people have a significant role in pushing up the numbers who suffer and die, or as ethnographer and researcher of natural disasters Roger Abbott puts it, 'turn[ing] ... natural hazard[s] into ... disaster[s]'.[5]

This impact of people in disasters was voiced by eighteenth-century philosopher Rousseau in response to Voltaire after the Lisbon earthquake. Perhaps part of the problem wasn't the kind of world we live in, but rather the actions, or inactions, of people. Rousseau wrote that 'Everything is good as it leaves the hands of the Author of things; everything degenerates in the hands of man.'[6]

According to this view, the problem is not with natural disasters per se, but with people. Humans add to the suffering and have become vulnerable to natural disasters in several different ways. What are some of the ways in which this has happened?

Global population growth

An article published by the World Health Organization highlights the impact that growing population sizes are having on the scale of natural disasters:

> Emergencies, especially those that occur in nature, only become catastrophic events when they combine with vulnerability factors, such as human settlements and population density. An earthquake occurring in a deserted area would be considered a natural hazard; but if it occurred in a megacity it would be recognized as a major disaster.[7]

Decreased mortality rates and longer lifespans, both resulting from better health care, have led to a quadrupling of the global population since the beginning of the twentieth century. More people have moved to cities, choosing to live in urban rather than rural spaces and in close proximity. By 2050, it is estimated that there will be between 9 and 10 billion people alive, many living in crowded conditions and competing for limited and increasingly strained natural resources. Robert White makes the point that more people are dying in disasters because there are more people alive than ever before.[8]

Moreover, the regions seeing the largest population growth are also those most prone to natural disasters. The Bay of Bengal is a case in point. Nearly 25% of all people alive today live in the countries bordering this periodically battered yet vast coastal region.[9] On one level a disaster will impact more people today than, say, a hundred years ago, simply because there are more people around.

Of course, global population increases are only part of an answer to this question. Human beings can also have a direct role in pushing up the death toll, and it is to this that we turn now.

Infrastructure

As many as 300,000 people were killed when the Bhola cyclone hit the coast of Bangladesh (then East Pakistan) in 1970, but the vast majority of these deaths could have been prevented. Typhoons, cyclones and hurricanes differ from other natural disasters in that they at least provide some warning of their arrival on weather maps, allowing time to respond. Yet poor telecommunication often prevents this vital news reaching those in the cyclone's path. Poor-quality roads further impede evacuation and lead to isolation of communities, especially those in rural areas. The combined result is that people are left stranded, without adequate shelter, and vulnerable not only to the cyclone but also to the famine and disease that follow in its wake.

After an equally devastating cyclone in 1991 in which almost 140,000 lost their lives, Bangladesh decided to shift their approach to cyclones from one of 'response and relief' to 'disaster risk reduction'.[10] Just over a thousand simple shelters were built or repaired along the coast and rural roads were improved. In 2007, a cyclone far stronger than Bhola hit, but this time fewer than 4,500 people died,[11] a hundredfold decrease compared with the deadly storm of 1970. Although cyclones cannot be prevented, unnecessary deaths can. Sometimes the scale of 'disaster' is skewed by human factors. There is much that governments and local authorities can do to improve disaster defences, ensuring that people are less vulnerable.

Poverty

When we hear of tens or hundreds of thousands being killed by a natural disaster, this is a sure sign that the region affected is one where there are significantly greater numbers living in poverty. According to one intergovernmental report, 95% of all natural-disaster-related deaths were in low-income countries.[12] The evidence is clear: poverty vastly increases a person's vulnerability to natural disasters.

To register this, we need only compare the impact of two similarly sized earthquakes, both of which occurred in densely populated areas. In October 1989, the San Francisco Bay Area was struck by a 7.1 magnitude earthquake, the largest since 1906. Loma Prieta took the lives of sixty-three people and injured 3,800 others. In contrast, a 7.0 magnitude quake struck Port-au-Prince, Haiti, in January 2010, killing up to 250,000 people and displacing 300,000.[13]

Why was the Haiti death toll three orders of magnitude greater than that of California? A number of causes are attributed to the vast difference in loss between these two seismically similar events. The most important reason is that Haitian buildings were not built to withstand earthquakes. Poorly built homes, schools, hotels and office blocks became death traps as they crumbled under the force of the tremors. When building regulations are ignored and corners are cut to save time and money, both exacerbated by corruption, then the suffering is ratcheted up. Those in poverty are always the greatest affected, with little choice over where or how they live. We are beginning to see that there is no such thing as a purely 'natural' disaster. People and nature both play a part. Natural evil and moral evil are always woven together.

And even when the disaster occurs in wealthier countries, those with the lowest incomes are still affected the hardest and for the longest. In Marjory's words, 'The neighbourhood you lived in determined how you fared in a hurricane.' When Katrina swept through New Orleans, 1,833 people lost their lives. Robert White points out that

> they were disproportionately the elderly, the infirm and the poor who had no cars and could not leave the city as the storm approached. The evacuation plans called for people to use their own cars to drive away from the coastal areas at risk of flooding. That worked well for 80–90 per cent of the residents of New Orleans. But 112,000 people without access to personal vehicles were stranded.[14]

It seems that, whatever the reasons behind a natural disaster, the fact that *so many* people die is usually because of human factors. Poverty is preventable. Poorly built tower blocks are preventable, and as one article on Haiti pointed out, 'Better buildings would have saved lives.'[15]

So we begin to see that although natural disasters have the potential to be lethal, people undoubtedly have the ability to turn them into even bigger catastrophes. However vulnerable we might be to natural disasters, we are made more vulnerable to them through the action or inaction of other people. Corruption, injustice and neglect, driven by greed and folly, certainly ramp up the numbers of people who suffer. And those in poverty are always worst off.

Climate change

During the twentieth century, the earth's global temperature has notably increased, bringing with it a pronounced effect on our experience of natural disasters. First, polar ice caps are melting, causing a global rise in sea levels, which, without intervention, could swell by a further half-metre by 2050.[16] A rise of 1 metre would be catastrophic and put millions of people at risk of coastal inundation,[17] flooding, displacement and disease. A *National Geographic* article highlights the impact on people and the cumulative impact on other kinds of natural disaster:[18]

> When sea levels rise as rapidly as they have been, even a small increase can have devastating effects on coastal habitats farther inland, it can cause destructive erosion, wetland flooding, aquifer and agricultural soil contamination with salt, and lost habitat for fish, birds, and plants . . .
>
> Already, flooding in low-lying coastal areas is forcing people to migrate to higher ground, and millions more are vulnerable from flood risk and other climate change

effects. The prospect of higher coastal water levels threatens basic services such as Internet access, since much of the underlying communications infrastructure lies in the path of rising seas.

Deluges may be the least dramatic of the natural disasters, but they are certainly one of the deadliest. More people are thought to die through the effects of flooding than from any other kind of natural disaster.

Second, increased land temperatures are causing wildfires to burn hotter, for longer and more often. Australia suffers fires every year, and even the Arctic burns in the summer, which ought to give us cause for concern.[19] Each time a fire sweeps through, millions of tons of 'planet-warming' carbon dioxide are emitted back into the atmosphere, and so the cycle continues. Climatologists believe that by 2070, more than 3 billion people could be living in conditions of extreme heat, enduring *average* temperatures of around 29°C.[20]

Third, higher surface water temperatures are causing increased numbers of hurricanes, leading to changes in local weather patterns.[21] Warmer water is also known to intensify storms, slow them down and increase rainfall. The forecast of slower hurricanes may, at first glance, seem like good news, as they might be thought to reap less havoc than faster ones. Not so. When a storm arrives on land it tends to fizzle out, as was the case with Hurricane Harvey in 2017, but warm water has a turbocharging effect. Reduced speed enables more water to be offloaded onto towns and villages, leading to more severe flooding and landslides. Ultimately, global warming will render hurricanes, typhoons and cyclones more destructive than ever.

Few would question the accelerating rise in global temperatures today, and a large majority of scientists are without doubt that human factors have played a key role. Excessive burning of fossil fuels such as coal, oil and gas has released vast quantities of heat-trapping carbon dioxide into the atmosphere, leading to a greenhouse effect on the earth. An article in the scientific journal *Nature* in 2019, drawing from data provided by the Intergovernmental Panel on Climate Change (IPCC), insisted that the earth's climate was very close to a 'tipping point' of irreversible damage.[22] Prior to COP26, hosted by the UK in 2021, the UN released a report, again from the IPCC, describing the situation as being 'code red' but stating that governments are not taking anywhere near enough action to limit the rise in temperatures to 1.5 degrees.[23] Urgent action is needed. Governments are in a position to limit the severity of future hurricanes, storms and flooding, but choose not to act. Millions of people, mostly those living in poverty, will be more vulnerable to disasters as a result.

Nature's signs

A BBC article on animal behaviour in the run-up to natural disasters highlights that, even when early warning technologies have failed, creatures of all kinds have started behaving very strangely, as if they knew something was about to happen. The report describes the 'minutes and hours' before the 2004 Indian Ocean tsunami:

Elephants ran for higher ground, flamingos abandoned low-lying nesting areas, and dogs refused to go outdoors.

In the coastal village of Bang Koey in Thailand, locals reported a herd of buffalo by the beach suddenly pricking their ears, gazing out to sea, then stampeding to the top of a nearby hill a few minutes before the tsunami struck.

'Survivors also reported seeing animals, such as cows, goats, cats and birds, deliberately moving inland shortly after the earthquake and before the tsunami came ... Many of those who survived ran along with these animals or immediately after.'[24]

Could it be that there are signs of nature that animals are aware of but humans aren't? The solar eclipse of 1999 revealed some interesting and slightly comical bird activity. Once the sun became almost entirely obscured, I remember being surprised at the loss not just of light but also heat. A warm summer's day very quickly became chilly, so much so that the local birds assumed that morning had once more arrived and began singing the dawn chorus all over again.

Observations of animal responsiveness to nature are not new – they are documented as far back as Ancient Greece, and of course beg the question why people don't have the same ability. Was there once a connection to nature that has been lost along the way, or are we meant to live in 'harmony' with the creatures and take our cues from them?

Or perhaps the crux is that we can choose to ignore nature's signs in ways that animals cannot? After all, the signs thrown out are not that subtle. Of all the kinds of natural disasters, volcanoes give the most warning. Yet, prior to the eruption of Vesuvius in AD 79, the inhabitants of Pompeii continued their lives, seemingly oblivious to the repeated coughing and spluttering of the nearby cone-shaped mountain. Only when ash began to rain down on them did they decide to evacuate, by which time it was far too late. Some natural disasters send warnings that humans can choose to heed or ignore. Our animal counterparts, on the other hand, seem 'wired' to respond to the signals around them. We can't rule out that our inability to read nature's signs is another factor that increases our vulnerability to natural disasters.

Why do so many people die in natural disasters? Some theologians and philosophers argue that the problem isn't with the natural world or how it has been arranged. The problem is with people. We turn disasters into catastrophes. In the wake of a disaster, there are always stories of how governments and authorities failed to heed warning signs, or to inform or educate people; or they underestimated the strength of nature's forces, or overestimated the sufficiency of existing protection; or they failed to implement the full range of protection available, or neglected to send humanitarian aid. Add to these the longer-term impacts of population growth, poverty and failure to care for the earth's habitat. As a result, many are, and will be, left more vulnerable to natural disasters than they need be.

This isn't the whole story, and other angles will be presented in later chapters. But it is certainly a large part of the story. The problem isn't so much that nature is broken or faulty, but that people are broken, or our connection to nature is broken, and as a result, we are all more vulnerable to the forces of nature.

Wildfires, Australia 2019–20

Stewart, regional manager for Billy Graham Rapid Response Team Chaplains

The fires of 2019–20 that covered much of Australia are seen once in a generation. Of course, there are outbreaks every year, but we haven't had firestorms like that since the 1980s or 90s. As regional manager for Samaritan's Purse chaplains in Australia and New Zealand, I was on the road for the whole of summer, from August to March.

We started in a little town called Stanthorpe in Queensland. The whole region had been drought-stricken for years. Everything was sun-scorched, plus there were very high winds and searing temperatures. Imagine a fire that can race towards a town at about 50 mph, and that's basically what Stanthorpe and nearby Tenterfield faced. Plain land fires with nothing in front of them to stop them. No natural features, no forests to slow them down, just open grassland fires.

The fire brigade couldn't get ahead of them, despite using aerial firefighting. When the fire reached the outskirts of the town it ran into short, mowed grass – lawns – that can be burned up in an instant. The flames whipped round the outskirts of the town at such speed that structures such as steel panel fences had no heat scorching on them at all. The fire was moving too fast to damage anything apart from grass. Residents were left shocked and bewildered. This travelling inferno was upon them and gone before they'd had time to register. Beyond the grassland we faced the bigger problem of the forests, which generate a much hotter, more ferocious kind of fire that incinerates everything in its path.

When fire hits a forest, it slows down and 'stands up', forming flames of up to 30 metres high. Much more heat is generated, thriving on dead timber and dry eucalyptus leaves which build up on the forest floor over time. Eucalyptus leaves and sap also contain their own flammable oil, which vaporizes when hot and burns easily. So, when a really big fire comes through a forest every fifteen to twenty years, it is devastating. This particular fire destroyed an area of 100–200 miles, leaving nothing but matchsticks for trees. And people live in those forests, wanting an undisturbed existence away from urban life.

Of course, with forest fires, flame height isn't the problem. The real problem is thermal radiation: the energy ahead of the fire that causes everything to smoulder before the fire itself hits. A fire at 1000°C, which is quite normal, can kill you at 100 metres away because of thermal radiation. We lose people every year who think they can outrun the fire, or try to drive through it to escape. What kills people in those situations is asphyxiation. The fire consumes all the oxygen in the air, so they can't breathe and pass out, causing the car to crash and burn.

For eight to ten weeks, we did not see stars at all, and it was like living in smog. Everything smelt of smoke, including our clothes. Looking upwards, we saw smudgy greyness, giving the impression that a veil had been drawn across the sky. The sun was visible but it was red, like in a sunset, from morning to dusk. We got used to it, but it was another reminder that the fires weren't out yet. Danger was still out there.

There was one firestorm that actually created its own weather system, called a pyrocumulus event. When there is so much heat and energy, the wind rushes in from every side and it creates a huge column like a chimney of smoke that rises and rises. Eventually, the moisture being carried upwards begins to freeze. Hail and cold rain start plummeting back down through the middle of the column, causing it to collapse, and sending shock waves shooting out across the ground. On one occasion, a fire truck beneath the column was thrown sideways and sent rolling with such force that the people inside were killed.

Some ask what the causes of wildfires are. Both human and natural causes play a major part in fires. One rural fire service leader was asked on national television about how wildfires start. He responded like this: 'There are four things that start fires: lightning, children, men and women.' Hot, dry weather and lightning play a part, but so do kids playing with matches.

There's a debate going on between conservationists who want to leave the forests alone to manage themselves, and the firefighters who want to be more interventionist and have controlled winter fires every two years to keep the fuel load down. After all, the firefighters have to stand in front of the full fury of the blaze coming from an out-of-control forest fire, and no-one wants to do that if it can be avoided. There's a huge difference between a fire that begins when lightning ignites a source and runs its course, and one that thrives on the prevailing weather conditions of strong winds and searing heat.

Controlled winter fires could also make a difference to forest regeneration. These really hot summer fires don't just burn everything above ground, they burn all the nutrients in the soil as well, to a depth of about half a metre. Cooler winter fires, on the other hand, can burn up the fuel on the ground without damaging the soil's nutrients, enabling the forest to regenerate more quickly. Cooler fires also have some natural benefits. Eucalyptus seed pods on the forest floor are ripened and open because of fire. There are plants that thrive in the aftermath, growing shoots and flowers even before the grass starts to regenerate.

Much of our work was with local communities, helping people practically in the aftermath of a disaster: tidying up, cutting down trees, washing out houses and so on. We try to get there and be present as soon as the door opens; as soon as the police pull the roadblocks out of the way.

All kinds of scenes confronted us as we went in to help. One couple had dragged a caravan onto their property just so they had something to sleep in. It was six weeks earlier that the fire had passed through, but they'd had no emotional energy to do anything about the mess, or the rubble of their home. We turned up with a team of six people and spent two to three hours arranging piles of debris into glass, metal, brickwork, burnt timber and so on. We took chainsaws and began chopping up trees to make room on the ground for them to bring in equipment and materials to begin the rebuilding.

Towards the end of our time, I sat with them and gave them space to tell their story, just listening and asking questions. In the space of an hour they went from sitting hunched and looking at the ground, to looking around – eyes bright – and smiling and laughing. The experience of being able to share their grief and shock sparked an incredible turnaround for them as a couple. They had energy to face what needed to be done. All we did was tidy up a bit, by no means getting everything finished. But that was enough to get them started.

Another guy, on the other side of town, had been living in a metal shipping container. The fire had come through and melted virtually everything inside, including the weatherproof seals. Inside the container, everything was black and smelt of burnt rubber. Its occupant was sitting in all the mess with nothing but a camping table, a couple of chairs and an umbrella. That was his world. My role as a chaplain was to spend time with him and let him know that help was available if he wanted it. We helped him clean up a little and bring some order to his chaos.

The reality is that, all too often, the fire is only the latest thing to happen. We hear all the time of people having only just buried a loved one when the fire hit. Or of others with inoperable cancer but no home left to die in. We met one couple whose house had burned while they were away getting treatment for the husband. The wife couldn't bring the husband home because everything had been smoke-damaged and the property was a mess. So our team spent a week clearing the driveways, removing a big gum tree that had fallen down beside the house, and chopping and clearing the timber and debris. We helped restore some normality for the husband so that he could return and recover. The wife was completely baffled that a bunch of people from all walks of life and from across Australia had come and worked hard in Jesus' name. We weren't doing it to earn brownie points; we weren't doing it to earn favour with any deity. We are loved already and want to demonstrate that love to others in a way that recognizes dignity, meets need and brings hope that there could be a better tomorrow.

There are moments when I scratch my head and wonder what God is doing. Sometimes I think he could have intervened. God could have blown the wind the other way. In some cases he did. On one occasion, the fire was racing towards two small towns in New South Wales – Pambula and Mallacoota – trapping them on the coast. Embers, lumps of flaming ash and coal, had started raining down, a sure sign that the fire was no more than 3 miles away. You can't fight an ember storm. The fragments just land everywhere, carried by the wind. As the fire got closer, the wind grew stronger and stronger, ash fell faster and then the heat came. The sky went black as if it was the middle of the night. People were cornered on the beach and in the sea, as a wall of fire around 20 metres high raced towards them at about 55 mph. Certain death was a matter of minutes away. Christians from the town started crying out to God, asking him to turn the wind. All of a sudden, the wind did something it shouldn't have done. Something it wasn't forecast to do. It changed direction, saving the town and the lives of the people in it, and making news headlines.[1] Some were calling it a miracle, including some with no previous belief in God.

4

Are natural disasters the judgment of God?

On hearing of a natural disaster, many are keen to offer their interpretation of events. Some are quick to pronounce the catastrophe as God's judgment on a particular region for a particular sin committed there. The Lisbon earthquake of 1755 was no exception. Many at that time read deep significance into the timing of the devastation, which began on the morning of All Saints' Day when many were in church; even those following God were doomed to destruction, let alone those who weren't. A Jesuit priest offered this perspective: 'Learn, O Lisbon, that the destroyers of our houses, palaces, churches and convents, the cause of death of so many people and of the flames that devoured such vast treasures are your abominable sins.'[1]

Responses of this kind are voiced after every major natural disaster. Some Muslim preachers interpreted the December 2004 tsunami as a judgment against the sex industry in largely Buddhist Thailand.[2] Other Christian preachers countered that it was levelled against Sumatra because of how believers have been treated in that region.[3] Hurricane Katrina was interpreted as a judgment on hedonistic New Orleans and for its failure to properly care for those in poverty. Rugby union star Israel Folau pronounced the 2019–20 bushfires a punishment for Australia's recent legalization of abortion and gay marriage.[4]

What are we to make of this perspective? Are natural disasters the judgment of God? Are some nations or regions singled out or specially targeted for punishment? There are problems with this view, not least the apparently indiscriminate way in which people's fate is 'decided'. We saw in chapter 1 how, in the aftermath of the 2004 tsunami, one journalist described how a line in the sand marked how far inland the water had come and delineated who had survived and who hadn't.[5] All kinds of people on the wrong side of the line perished, regardless of their religion and reputation in society. Naturalists argue that the widespread impact of a disaster is further evidence that spiritual explanations are futile here.[6] The forces of nature do not 'choose' their victims, they merely sweep away whatever is in their path. Martin Kettle, writing in *The Guardian*, put it like this:

> Certainly the giant waves generated by the quake made no attempt to differentiate between the religions of those whom it made its victims. Hindus were swept away in India, Muslims were carried off in Indonesia, Buddhists in Thailand. Visiting Christians and Jews received no special treatment either. This poses no problem for the scientific belief system. Here, it says, was a mindless natural event, which destroyed Muslim and Hindu alike.[7]

Many Christians would agree that the apportioning of blame is futile. Natural disasters are not God's judgment on a particular community, city or nation. They are the result of living in a complex and broken world. Reading too much into who survives and who doesn't, and why, only adds to the pain for survivors trying to come to terms with their loss.

Every time a large disaster strikes, there are stories of tragedy as well as stories of extraordinary protection and rescue of people from every religion and no religion. In one Indonesian town, the entire Christian population had retreated to the mountains to celebrate Christmas and escaped the Boxing Day deluge as a result. But I also learned of how entire missionary families were killed. One story told of how many sheltering in a mosque were saved, but another story told of how a young Muslim man's entire family were killed having celebrated a wedding days earlier. Did some deserve to survive and others not?

Moreover, whatever the misdemeanours of the place in question, there are always babies and young children among the victims who have surely not been alive long enough to contribute good or evil to society as a whole. Are they to be punished for the wrongs of others? If God exists, is this how he works? Does he deal out miscarriages of justice, punishing infants for the crimes of men and women?

A judgment claim is tantamount to saying that one particular place or region was *more deserving* of disaster than others. But is this really the case? In the wake of pronouncements of divine punishment after the 1755 Lisbon earthquake, Voltaire argued that he could name any number of European cities that were certainly no better than Lisbon and very possibly worse. Take Paris or London, for example.

Seeing this mass of victims, will you say,
'God is avenged. Their death is the price of their
   crimes'?

What crime, what fault had the young committed,
Who lie bleeding at their mother's breast?
Did fallen Lisbon indulge in more vices
Than London or Paris, which live in pleasure?
Lisbon is no more, but they dance in Paris.[8]

Whenever one city is afflicted, there are always numerous others whose deeds make them seem even more qualified for judgment. Indeed, is there a place on earth that is totally innocent?

Biblical disasters

The view that natural disasters represent judgment is perhaps offered because there are instances in the Bible in which God does appear to bring judgment on regions or nations at certain times. And he does so partly through natural disasters. The most famous and dramatic of these is Noah's flood, in which God is said to have wiped out all people in the known world because of rampant and widespread evil.[9] We could also bring to mind the destruction of the cities of Sodom and Gomorrah, brought about by seeming seismic activity and by raining down burning sulphur on these cities.[10] The plagues of blood, frogs, gnats, flies, boils, hail, locusts and darkness, the plague on livestock and the death of every firstborn male were inflicted on Egypt for its worship of false gods and for refusing to let the people of Israel go free.[11] The most severe earthquake in Israel's history (c.760 BC) was predicted two years previously, by the prophet Amos, and taken as a judgment on Israel and its neighbours for walking away from God and for allowing horrendous evil and injustice to run unchecked.[12]

In the past, in some cases, natural disasters do seem to have been a conduit for divine judgment.

However, it would be misplaced to extrapolate this thinking to all disasters today. Pastor and author Erwin Lutzer draws a distinction between the time when God made himself known mainly to a specific people group, the Israelites, living in a particular place, the land of Israel,[13] and our current era. In the former era, the physical land was paramount, and therefore some of the ways in which God interacted with his people were by means of their locality and geography. Today, however, things are different. The life, death and resurrection of Jesus ushered in a new era, the age of the Spirit, in which God is present to people not based on nationality or geography but on belief in and devotion to Jesus Christ.

There are also instances of natural disasters in the Bible that are not interpreted in a spiritual way. They simply happen according to the forces of nature. Hurricanes and storms are recorded, such as the one that rendered the apostle Paul shipwrecked on Malta instead of sailing to Rome. There were dozens onboard, but no lives were lost.[14] Numerous famines due to crop failure are also recorded,[15] such as the seven-year famine during the life of Joseph.[16] Joseph even had prior warning of the crop failure to come. A dream of Pharaoh's revealed there would be seven years of plenty followed by seven years of famine, and Joseph used his position of influence to store up grain during the years of abundance, so that many lives could be saved during the years of little. In each case, the emphasis was on responding to the disaster and providing for the injured and sick, rather than offering a spiritual interpretation and leaving people to their fate.

Finally, there are instances in the Bible where a spiritual interpretation of a disaster is warranted, but not in a negative way. In some instances, natural disasters are a pointer to the power and majesty of God. For example, the giving of the Ten Commandments to Moses on Mount Sinai was accompanied by thunder, lightning and a violent earthquake, each serving as a reminder of God's holiness and sovereignty over people and nature. Similarly, poetic references to earthquakes and volcanoes feature in some of the psalms (see chapter 5) and these phenomena are to be seen not as conduits of judgment but rather as awe-inspiring reminders of the God who made the whole natural world.

Jesus on disasters

The closest we come to hearing Jesus respond to larger-scale suffering is when he is told about an atrocity against some Galileans at the hands of their Roman oppressors, and then discusses the collapse of a tower in Siloam:

> Now there were some present at that time who told Jesus about the Galileans whose blood Pilate had mixed with their sacrifices. Jesus answered, 'Do you think that these Galileans were worse sinners than all the other Galileans because they suffered this way? I tell you, no! But unless you repent, you too will all perish. Or those eighteen who died when the tower in Siloam fell on them – do you think they were more guilty than all the others living in Jerusalem? I tell you, no! But unless you repent, you too will all perish.'[17]

It is not clear whether the tower collapsed because of an earthquake or some other force of nature, or because of shoddy workmanship. But either way, Jesus is addressing the elephant in the room and the opinion of some around him: *Were the people who died worse than the rest of us?*

His answer couldn't be clearer: 'I tell you, no!' The Galileans were not worse sinners. The Siloam victims were not more guilty. They had not been singled out. We can't read too much into the fact that it was them and not us. But there is also a sobering 'but' that follows: 'But unless you repent, you too will all perish.'

It's as though Jesus is saying to them, *You are not less guilty, either. They were not worse, but you are not better.* Jesus is saying that all are guilty and vulnerable to the same fate. All have lived in ways that displease God and fall short of his standards. As a result, when hearing about large-scale loss of life, it should not provoke a diagnosis of the spiritual state of other people, but rather a realistic assessment of ourselves. It should set the spiritual focus inwards, not outwards.

Thinking more broadly, atrocities and disasters are not to be interpreted as judgments on particular people for particular wrongs. These are tragic events, and we must do all in our power to help victims and prevent them from happening the next time. But disasters also have something to say to onlookers. They serve as a reminder that life on earth is brief, that human life is precious, and that it can be over in an instant, with no warning.

If I were to die tomorrow, what would my ultimate fate be? Some believe death is the end, and oblivion awaits. Others believe that there is life beyond the grave. Christians believe that all people will be raised and then each will undergo judgment. Each person will answer to God for their life on earth: for the things done, said and thought, both good and bad. In other words, natural disasters are not the judgment of God, but they are a sobering reminder that one day judgment will come to us all.

Signs of the times

Later, Jesus goes on to say that, as time progresses, there will be increasing numbers of large-scale disasters around the world:

> Nation will rise against nation, and kingdom against kingdom. There will be great earthquakes, famines and pestilences in various places, and fearful events and great signs from heaven ... There will be signs in the sun, moon and stars. On the earth, nations will be in anguish and perplexity at the roaring and tossing of the sea.[18]

These verses are describing great turmoil that can be interpreted on many different levels and be relevant to many different time periods in history. They indicate that, as history progresses, there will continue to be both natural and man-made disasters, and possibly with increasing frequency and severity. The biblical story is clear that at some point in the future, time and space as we know them will come to an end. 'End' of course may still refer to hundreds of thousands of years, but cosmologically speaking, for a universe that is 14 billion years old, the end is coming soon. We are told not to be surprised by these things, nor fearful, but to be watchful and prayerful, and to stay focused on what really matters. In this way, natural disasters are signs and reminders that the earth itself is temporary, however permanent it may seem.

Angry God?

The idea of judgment can evoke images of an angry, vengeful God who delights in calamity and venting on people. Surely this is at odds with the notion of the loving God whom Christians speak about? In fact, the opposite is true. God judges *because* he is loving. It is not always wrong to be angry. When we hear about people dying unnecessarily from COVID-19, or of toddlers being abducted and killed, or of institutional racism, we get angry. Why? Because of our care and concern for those involved. It is good to be angry about the right things, and is an expression of love. In fact, to remain indifferent in the face of these evils is itself an evil.

God is not indifferent to evil and is clear that ultimately, evil will not go unchecked. Those who seem to have got away with heinous crimes will be subject to the justice of God. Hitler will answer to God. Human traffickers will answer to God. Corrupt leaders will answer to God. And every injustice, even miscarriages of justice, here on earth will be put right. God will set everything right. Justice will be done. No-one will dispute each verdict. And all because God is love; he does not simply turn a blind eye and let evil slide.

Of course, there is a flip side to this. What will be the verdict on my own life? I know I am capable of kindness, but also callousness; of generosity, but also greed; of good thoughts, but also dark ones that seemingly come from nowhere. I may not have committed the crimes of a dictator, but I am also far from the person I want to be, even with my best efforts. Therefore, justice is needed for the things I have said, for the way I have treated people, and for the good I have left undone. It is sobering indeed. And every human being who has ever lived is answerable in the same way, including Mother Teresa and Florence Nightingale. This is where it starts to get really difficult. If God must bring absolute justice for things open and hidden, seen and unseen, actions, words *and thoughts*, then how is it possible for anyone to know the love of God?

There is a way through

The prairies of North America are vulnerable to wildfires every year and a method traditionally used by householders was to burn the grass around the perimeter of their property. They fostered a controlled fire not unlike the winter forest fires of the Australian outback that Stewart spoke of. When a big wildfire eventually blew through and came close to homes, it would meet with charred stubble, run out of fuel and stall. Because an earlier fire had already burned through, house-holders were protected from a greater, more damaging furnace.[19]

This can help us to understand something of what God has done for us in Jesus. No-one who trusts and follows Jesus need fear the judgment and justice of God. We are spared his justice because Jesus has borne the brunt of it for us already. On the cross, the 'heat' that should rightly consume us all for our wrongdoing or 'sin' was instead borne by Jesus. As a result, we are free to walk across the charred stubble to know the love and friendship of God. There is a way through judgment for us. Somehow, both the love and the justice of God are satisfied by Christ's death on the cross. Sin yields consequences and ultimately death, but Jesus, who is without sin, has carried our sins for us to the grave. The need for justice has been satisfied, meaning that we are free again to know the love of God if we would like to. Jesus has rebuilt the bridge between people and God. Friendship with God is available to all. And all we have to do is ask; to take Jesus at his word and repent. To turn around and go in a new direction.

No-one is excluded from the love of God and, while each of us is alive on earth, it is never too late to turn back to him. The words of Jesus, that 'unless you repent, you too will all perish', may appear direct and stark, but the truth is that to give a warning where there is genuine danger is actually a kindness. When we see warnings at roadsides alerting us to falling rocks or sharp bends; or warnings near electricity pylons warning of the danger of electric shock; or even the multiple warnings each day that a parent gives their child, these are not simply to nag or oppress or impose a feeling of fear or unworthiness. Rather they are to highlight danger so that disaster can be prevented – in this case, the cataclysm of being without God's love for ever. God has shown kindness in alerting us to the need to repent and be put right with him. He has also *delayed* this ultimate day of reckoning,[20] to allow more time for people to take stock, look at their lives and choose how they will respond. Disasters today are not God's judgment, but they certainly focus our attention on what really matters.

Taal Volcano eruptions,
Philippines 1977, 2011 and 2020

Nilo, local resident

I first experienced a volcanic eruption when I was eleven years old. In the Philippines, we sit in the Pacific Ring of Fire, where there are five to six hundred volcanoes, thirty of which are active. The Taal Volcano, just 37 miles from Manila, is one of the most active volcanoes in the world and has erupted thirty-eight times since records began. In recent times, there has been activity every year.

At the time of the 1977 eruption, we were at school. I don't remember hearing an explosion, but it wasn't long before lessons were cancelled, and we were sent home for a few days. I didn't really understand what was happening. Pictures on TV showed the volcano erupting just 4 miles away, but all we could see was white ash falling everywhere. I spent days playing in this grey-white powder with my friends, watching it floating in the air and coming to rest, turning everything grey. I would listen to the sound of it tapping like rain drops on the iron sheet roofing of our house, especially at night. The roof ended up damaged by the sheer volume of ash.

I had a feeling of fear, but also enjoyed these days at home. But when my uncle's cattle died, I realized that this was serious, and that feeling of fear intensified. If the animals were dying, then it must be harmful to people. At that time, I had no idea the ash contained pyroclastic materials that are very dangerous for your lungs. No-one wore masks back then.

The Philippine Institute of Volcanology and Seismology, or PHIVOLCS, exists to monitor and provide updates on volcanic activity. It has equipment installed inside Taal itself and provides scientific data on things such as the number of tremors, the temperature of the water and activity in the crater. Changes in each of these things are monitored closely. PHIVOLCS has also generated a hazard map for the whole country, and so anyone buying property today can check where the fault lines are and avoid them.

A national disaster law was introduced in the Philippines in 2011 as part of our response to the many natural and man-made disasters we encounter. There is also a national disaster risk reduction management council, which is responsible for implementing this law. The problem is that local governments are not prepared to play their part. There is a policy stating that 5% of the local budget should go into disaster preparation and response, but this still doesn't seem to help. The province or region housing the Taal Volcano is wealthy compared with others, but they don't allocate enough money and resources to getting ready. People who are living in the communities near the volcano do not easily believe the PHIVOLCS warning that an eruption is imminent. When an eruption does finally happen, the Government ask why they weren't warned. They had tons of warnings but chose to ignore them.

I have my opinions as to why this happens. One reason is because we simply have so many natural disasters, with as many as twenty typhoons each year and constant volcanic activity. The Government can't respond to everything and needs to prioritize. Another reason is that the Government know that people do not want to leave their homes. Local people have seen it all before. Having survived many eruptions so far, they won't agree to evacuate unless an eruption is clearly taking place in front of them. The challenge is this: how do you encourage disaster preparedness when the people are living in the midst of one natural disaster after another? Perhaps the best preparation is to know how to protect yourself when it happens.

On 12 January 2020, Taal erupted again. This time we saw the ash plumes in Manila, 37 miles away. The evacuation, which ought to cover a 7-mile radius, was delayed for several days, and people died as a result. Provision was minimal, even in this economically wealthy province. For example, a centre housing three thousand evacuees had only one toilet, and it really broke my heart to see that. A day or two later, a lot of help came from the private sector. Social media has made a big difference, and news travels very quickly now. People living in Metro Manila brought supplies by car. I was one of them, and drove to visit friends and relatives, this time bringing face masks to protect from the pyroclastic materials in the air. Ash had fallen as far away as Manila, but it was especially deep approaching my village (10 to 15 cm). Immediately my mind raced back to when I was an eleven-year-old boy, but this time I was able to recognize what was happening. The ash rain, the noise on the roof. The sky was full for nine days.

There are people who live on the volcanic island itself, and since one of the two lakes is a volcanic crater, they essentially live on the volcano. Three or four villages worth of people, with an elected chairman. Roughly a thousand people. One thing that really puzzles me is that somehow they were able to secure a certificate of ownership of some of this land. I ask myself, how exactly has it happened that people have come to own part of a volcano? It's unthinkable, but it has really happened in Taal. We call it an open secret.

A couple from my church hosted eleven families comprising sixty-six people from the island itself after the 2020 eruption. I asked them why they were living on the volcano. Wouldn't it be better to be at a safer distance? Their answer? They have lived there for a long time and have learned to recognize the signs of an eruption. They don't wait for the PHIVOLCS announcement. When birds start migrating, dogs start barking and cats make funny noises, they know it's time to leave. Even the cockroaches: when they start coming out of cracks and crevices, they know it's time to get away from there. Cockroaches like cold temperatures and dark places, so when they come out into the light something must be going on. By learning to recognize signs like these, no-one from this community has ever died.

There are also benefits to living close to a volcano. It is good from an agricultural point of view because the land is very fertile. Produce such as pineapple and rice grow well there. It's also a popular tourist spot. People take a boat ride across the lake, boil eggs in the hot springs, and take a horse ride to the second crater. Aside from farming, the local people earn extra money from tourism.

There could also be an economic benefit because the cost of land in the Philippines is very expensive and risky areas are more affordable. Political agendas are not impossible either.

Three villages is close to a thousand voters and the regional government may prefer to have their vote than force them to move to a safer region.

When I ask people why they think these disasters keep happening to us in the Philippines, one theme that keeps coming up is that these are signs of the return of Christ, the belief that one day Jesus Christ will return to this earth to judge the living and the dead and to make all things new. Even the fortune-tellers mention the second coming. We call it folk Catholicism or folk Christianity. Natural disasters cause people to pause. To watch ash and dust falling outside from the comfort of your own home is a thought-provoking experience. An experience you need to assess.

The concept of God punishing us through volcanic eruptions and typhoons is also very strong. You hear about it everywhere, from the churches to village gatherings, and from young and old. Some say we're being punished for the drug wars in the Philippines that have killed as many as thirty thousand. People have their different explanations. Yet the Bible says that '[God] causes his sun to rise on the evil and the good, and sends rain on the righteous and the unrighteous' (Matt. 5:45). Natural disasters don't select their victims; everyone is affected. A calamity such as a volcanic eruption or typhoon does not discriminate, but has an impact on all people, regardless of what they believe or how they are living.

5

Can science now answer all of our questions?

I will never forget the day I climbed a live volcano. For roughly two-thirds of our 1500-metre, five-hour ascent up the classical cone that is Volcán Villarrica, we needed crampons and ice picks. It was autumn in southern Chile, but soon enough the ice was melted by the furnace beneath our feet. As we neared the summit, we had fine volcanic ash underfoot that gave way with each step, warmed by the heat from this mountain that was more than just a mountain. Reaching the crater itself, coughing away the sulphurous fumes and covering our mouths, we were able to walk around and move close to the main vent. I inched forward and peered over the edge, gazing in awe and with some fear at the molten lava hundreds of metres below. That was in 2001. Villarrica erupted again in 2015.

There are roughly ten thousand volcanoes on earth, around a hundred of which are active. They rightly deserve a healthy respect and have made their mark on the history books numerous times. Mount Vesuvius buried the cities of Pompeii and Herculaneum in lava and ash in AD 79, and remains active today.[1] Soberingly, some volcanologists believe Vesuvius is still to do its worst. We could also look at the eruption of Krakatoa in Sumatra in 1883, considered to be one of the worst cataclysms in modern history. Over thirty-six thousand people were killed, and so much ash spewed into the atmosphere that countries and continents were deprived of their usual warm weather. A similarly devastating eruption in 1815 is said to have led to 'the year without a summer'[2] in the northern hemisphere. More recently, in 1980, Washington State's Mount St Helens erupted with, in the words of one writer, 'the force of five hundred Hiroshima-sized atomic bombs', causing 'the biggest landslide in human history and [carrying] enough material to bury the whole of Manhattan to a depth of four hundred feet'.[3] Fifty-seven people were killed, some as far away as 18 miles.

Yet the volcano to end all others does not have a distinctive vent nor is it a mountain that can be climbed. Geologists came across its crater when NASA began taking photographs from space. Yellowstone National Park in Wyoming, USA, consisting of 2.2 million acres, *is itself* the crater of a super volcano. In the past it has erupted with a violence unknown to humans, and, geologically speaking, another eruption is due any day now.

Gods of nature?

Through Nilo's story we see the vital part that modern volcanology plays in our understanding of volcanic activity and our ability to predict eruptions. Through the work of centres such as PHIVOLCS we gain wonderful insight and understanding into the workings of these captivating, fire-breathing mountains and other kinds of seismic activity. Meteorology, similarly, has greatly aided our understanding and prediction of tropical storms and weather systems. What, then, do we do with the spiritual explanations posed in the past and that sometimes still feature today? After all, hurricanes are named after *Huracán*, the Mayan god of wind, fire and storms and one of the thirteen deities involved in the creation of human beings from corn, according to the Mayan tradition.[4] When provoked to anger, Huracán destroys everything in his path. Volcanoes are named after the Roman god of fire, *Vulcan*, of a not dissimilar temperament from Huracán.[5] The word 'typhoon' probably originates from the Greek *Typhos*, or *Typhon*, the most destructive of the Greek gods, whose anger was thought to underly volcanic activity and fierce storms.[6] One Greek mythology expert describes Typhon as

> the largest monster ever born. From the thighs downward he was nothing but coiled serpents, and his arms which, when he spread them out, reached a hundred leagues in either direction, had countless serpents' heads instead of hands. His brutish ass-head touched the stars, his vast wings darkened the sun, fire flashed from his eyes, and flaming rocks hurtled from his mouth.[7]

Yet in our modern age, scientific explanations are given in place of spiritual ones. Instead of flaming rocks hurtling from the mouth of Typhon, volcanologists inform us that molten magma issues through the main vent at the centre of a volcano. Instead of Typhon's vast wings causing the sun to darken, we learn that this happens because huge quantities of sulphurous rock and ash are expelled into the atmosphere, blocking out the light. The accompanying fire need not be explained by Typhon's eyes, but by the intense temperatures involved.

Scientific accounts have offered a more rational and informative take on natural disasters than simply chalking them down to the anger of the gods, and much benefit has come from our improved understanding and study of nature. But does this mean that the sciences can now answer all of our questions and God is no longer relevant?

Does Genesis 1 contradict science?

An assumption often made is that the pages of the Bible are in direct contradiction to the discoveries of science. But this is not the case. Looking closer we see that the opening verses of the Bible were written with the surrounding polytheistic culture in mind, the dominant belief of which was that there were many (hence 'poly') gods (hence 'theism'), each of whom had limited power over a particular force of nature, not unlike Vulcan, Typhon and Huracán. There were sun gods, moon gods, gods that controlled the stars. There were gods of water, sea, earth, fire and wind. Nature itself was considered divine.

The author of Genesis, on the other hand, took a very different view and expressed it right from the very first sentence, which reads, 'In the beginning God created the heavens and the earth.'[8] The author's view is monotheistic: in other words, that *one* (hence 'mono') *supreme God* exists who made the natural world and is sovereign over it and all of its elements and forces. God created the natural world but is himself distinct from it. Nature is not divine.

Much time has been spent discussing the first two chapters of Genesis to interpret what these verses tell us about the age of the earth, the means by which humans arrived on the scene, and how both are to be married with scientific accounts. Yet commentators such as David Wilkinson argue that these verses are not primarily about the 'how' or 'how long ago' of our world, but rather the 'who' behind it.[9]

Near Eastern Babylon and Mesopotamia had their own creation stories, such as *Enuma Elish* and *Marduk, Creator of the World*, which told of deities battling it out for supremacy over their spheres of influence. With this in mind, the author of Genesis sets out to say something quite different, albeit in a poetic style. What does he say? That one God exists who made and upholds the whole natural world *but himself is not resident within it*. The wind is not divine, the moon is not divine, volcanoes are not divine, and neither are hurricanes. God is divine and made everything around us. The world we enjoy did not come about on the whim of an angry deity, but rather is the purposeful work of one God, who loves and creates because it is in his character to do so. The author of Genesis makes this point in some very stark ways. For example, the sun and moon are referred to in the narrative as the 'greater light' and the 'lesser light', because to use the words 'sun' and 'moon' would have meant using words that deified them.[10]

To summarize, in the West we may have moved on from belief in gods of nature, but this does not mean that all religious beliefs are to be rejected. Rather, some beliefs are more persuasive than others in making sense of the forces of nature. A helpful question to be asking is, which belief system makes best sense of why science is possible in the first place?

How is science even possible?

The modern scientific revolution, which began in the sixteenth century, marked a shift from a polytheistic to a monotheistic outlook, which was pivotal to progress in this era. Why would this shift make such a difference? First, if nature is itself not seen as divine then there is a new permission to study it. Scientists are no longer trespassing on the territory of the gods but are simply investigating how the world works. Second, the unpredictability that comes from ascribing moods and personalities to the elements is removed, making way for a more ordered universe with only one chieftain rather than the chaos of many. In this kind of universe, laws and regularities might be expected and can be sought out by scientific endeavour. It was precisely this kind of monotheistic belief that inspired a number of important contributors to the modern scientific revolution, such as mathematician Isaac Newton (1643–1727), astronomer Johannes Kepler (1571–1630) and geneticist Gregor Mendel (1822–84). As author and apologist C. S. Lewis put it, 'Men became scientific because they expected law in nature, and they expected law in nature because they believed in a Legislator.'[11]

As a theology student I remember attending a lecture on science and the Christian faith. When we were considering the history of science, a slide was displayed that showed a long list of well-known scientists, each of whom held a belief in God. I remember staring at it in amazement, wondering why no-one had ever told me this before, and thinking that this was surely one of the world's best-kept secrets. The manner in which science is reported in the media and in popular and academic writing can often leave us thinking that belief in God is incompatible with science and is even a hindrance to scientific progress. Yet the history books tell us that the opposite is true. The belief that the laws of nature have been set in place by a 'lawgiver' actually provided the *foundation* for scientific study, and still does so today – arguably, much more so than the belief that those laws are the product of time plus matter plus chance. The view that nature is neither accidental nor volatile, but purposefully created and ordered by God, arguably provides the strongest basis for the scientific method.

Spiritual versus scientific perspectives

Have scientific explanations ruled out the need for God? Far from it. Belief in God adds to our understanding of reality. Take the e-commerce company Amazon, for example. Does having a good handle on the processes and procedures underlying Amazon rule out any need for belief in the existence of Jeff Bezos? Of course not. There are different *kinds of explanations* when it comes to Amazon, both of which can exist together. The processes and procedures provide essential infrastructure, and Jeff Bezos is the one who founded this company in 1994.

It is the same with God and science. Belief in a creator God who set the universe in motion some 14 billion years ago is in no way incompatible with the practice of science that seeks to uncover its workings. Spiritual perspectives can exist alongside scientific ones. In fact, both are needed for a more complete understanding of reality. Trying to make sense of Amazon using its processes alone will leave you with a limited understanding. To grasp the vision, history, oversight and everyday dealings of Amazon, you need to consider Bezos too.

Similarly, spiritual descriptions can also exist alongside scientific ones because the Bible was never intended to be a scientific textbook. There are different genres of writing in its pages, from creative writing to eyewitness accounts, narrative, songs and wise sayings. The opening chapters of Genesis are a form of creative writing describing events that happened in history, but not necessarily in a literal way. This means that we can listen to scientific expertise and the words of the Bible that together describe reality in mutually compatible ways.[12]

A new volcanic fissure recently opened up in Iceland, near Reykjavik,[13] and people rushed to see it for themselves despite being warned of the dangers. Locals and tourists stood watching for long periods, captivated by the red-orange lava spewing from what was just an ordinary mountainside days earlier. When no casualties are involved, there is something striking and awe-inspiring about the rawness of nature. There may even be instances of this in the Bible, where people have been struck by the majesty of nature and have interpreted it not just as beautiful but also as something that points to God. For example, in Psalm 97:5 we read,

The mountains melt like wax before the LORD,
before the Lord of all the earth.

Another instance is seen in Psalm 104:31–32:

May the glory of the LORD endure for ever;
may the LORD rejoice in his works –
he who looks at the earth, and it trembles,
who touches the mountains, and they smoke.

Waxy, melting, smoking mountains sound like volcanoes, although they could also refer to landslides. Alternatively, they could be taken non-literally; the 'levelling of mountains' is sometimes used to depict God shaking things up and putting them back in the right order. Either way, we can make two observations. First, these verses are not at odds with the work of volcanologists. They are poetic descriptions of natural phenomena that are inspired by a sense of awe and wonder at the world God has made. But room is still left for accounts of magma, vents, ash clouds and pyroclastic flow. Second, the psalmist doesn't see the beauty and majesty of nature as an end in itself; rather it points beyond itself to God, in much the same way that another psalmist concluded that,

> The heavens declare the glory of God;
> the skies proclaim the work of his hands.[14]

As we continue thinking about whether or not the sciences can answer all of our questions, we see here that even the most detailed scientific descriptions will always leave room for other perspectives, including spiritual ones. Scientific explanations are indispensable, but on their own they are insufficient to capture the whole range of human experience, or to give a complete picture of reality.

Deep questions

A final reason why science alone can't answer all of our questions is because we ask many questions that lie beyond the realm of science. Cosmologists give us detailed descriptions of the events surrounding the beginnings of our universe, but cosmology can't answer the question of why our universe exists in the first place. Why is there something rather than nothing? Neuroscientists give us elegant descriptions of the brain networks that are recruited in all manner of cognitive tasks. But neuroscience can't answer the question why we are conscious in the first place. Why can we think *at all*? Psychologists and sociologists may observe and document human behaviour, but their disciplines can't answer questions of meaning. Why am I here? What is the purpose of my life? Perhaps most importantly of all, the sciences can't answer the question of whether or not God exists, and whether or not this life is all that there is. Modern medicine and cosmetic advances may help some of us to delay death, but they provide no answer to whether or not Jesus rose from the dead.

Why does the universe exist? Why am I a conscious being? What is the purpose of my life? Does God exist? Did Jesus rise from the dead? These are all vital questions, some of which we may have found ourselves asking at various points in life. Yet they are questions that simply cannot be answered scientifically. We need to step beyond the realm of science to give them due consideration. Have you had the opportunity to ask your questions?

Drought and conflict, South Sudan 2006

Becks, Emergency Response WASH Manager

I was in Sudan (now South Sudan) for a total of four years and worked for two different organizations during that time. Initially, we were based in a place called Renk, in Upper Nile State right in the middle of South Sudan. The Continued Peace Agreement (CPA) had been signed in 2005 and the United Nations Development Programme (UNDP) were funding recovery projects within South Sudan. I went in 2006 as the Emergency Response WASH Manager – WASH standing for water, sanitation and hygiene. It was my first mission. I was very green and didn't really know what I was doing, but really believed that I was meant to go.

At the time, the fighting between the Muslim North and Christian South was still going on, as was the war in Darfur. Corruption was rife. The Government was not functioning and there were many internally displaced persons (IDPs) who had lost everything and were living hand-to-mouth in camps of anywhere between three hundred people and fifteen thousand people. Our role was to rehabilitate boreholes to provide a water supply, to build latrines in schools and to promote hygiene.

Two years later, I moved to work for an emergency response water and sanitation team that provided emergency latrines and water supply for people in camps. We were based in Juba in the south, but from there would move around to different locations, camping in our mosquito domes. Sometimes the emergency response required us to get in a boat and go down the river to help whole villages who were cut off from clean water because of the fighting. But we had to stop that when the fighting intensified.

After four years in South Sudan, I returned to the UK to work for Bristol Water. But when more fighting broke out in 2013, I took a month of unpaid leave to help with the emergency response. One day, we were working just outside a UN protection of civilians camp when fierce fighting broke out very close by, forcing everyone in the area to take refuge in the camp. There were tanks outside and reports of people being shot in hospital beds and in the streets. The mother of one of our staff members was shot for no reason other than that she was from a particular tribe. We were scared. But then the pump broke at the river and there was no water in the camp for nearly three days. None of the drivers wanted to set foot outside the camp because of the danger. It was really hard to feel so helpless. We were stuck there for a week, with no way of getting out. I've never known tribal conflict like it. Even inside the camp, different tribes would slash one another's water systems. Systems that we had built.

Finally, there was a ceasefire, and we were all evacuated on two UN planes, along with 80% of all humanitarians in South Sudan. There were twelve or thirteen NGO vehicles taking people to the airport, and as we were setting off, a boy of around ten or twelve asked me in Arabic, 'Where are you going?' I said, 'Oh, we're just going outside.' Half an hour later, he would have seen the two planes taking off and must've felt completely abandoned by us. I found that absolutely heartbreaking and remember crying all the way back to Juba. I've had to be evacuated several times over the years, and it's something that I really struggle with, because I don't get to make that decision. Someone else makes it for me. But I'm a stayer, and it's devastating to know that people need assistance but you can't do anything.

One week after being evacuated from that war zone I was a bridesmaid at a friend's wedding in the UK, and I really noticed the contrast with life in England. For a lot of aid workers, going home is the hardest part, because people back home don't really get it. In the UK, we have everything we need: a roof over our heads, water, food and electricity. In Sudan, the whole of life is about securing these things. People walk, collect water and cook to feed their families. The next day they do the same things all over again.

People in Sudan just accept their suffering. Women die in labour all the time because they don't have access to health care. I think about my family and friends back in England who've had complications during childbirth and realize that, in South Sudan, they would have died. Every family has had at least one child die in childbirth or of some disease. They say it's normal and just part of life, but even so it always feels wrong. It's devastating for them, but you don't hear them getting angry with God. They accept what's happening, and they have hope that things will get better.

There was one boy who had polio. I think his name was Moses. His parents knew he needed to go to the hospital, but it was a three-day walk away. The mother was looking after five other children and the father worked away, so they had to wait. A lot of time passed before they were finally able to find the time and money to go, but by then the boy was so ill that he couldn't walk. Yet they went. And they walked for three days. People in South Sudan are walkers – tall and amazingly strong. Incredibly, the boy made a full recovery, but in the meantime it must have been heartbreaking for the parents to see their child get more and more ill, and not be able to do anything about it. This kind of story is common. There are many children in similar situations who die.

During my initial four years in South Sudan, I had given up hope because I didn't think I'd succeeded in making a difference. There were already Sudanese pump mechanics who knew exactly how to fix the water supply. All they needed were spare parts and a car to travel between the different boreholes, but the Government preferred to rely on NGOs to provide these. They didn't really need me there, and I also knew that in six months' time a borehole could well be broken again. I knew it was time to leave because if I'd given up hope, then I wasn't able to give hope to other people. I had been in the role for too long.

That's when I learnt that it's really about the individual. If a borehole being fixed for six months meant that one child wouldn't die because he or she got clean water, then that's what I had to focus on. I had to learn that I wasn't there to help the whole of South Sudan, even though I wanted to. It really humbled me to think that I could be there just to help one person or one community. The need is so big that it can be overwhelming.

There was one time when we drilled fourteen or fifteen boreholes only to discover that eleven of them were completely dry. I remember asking, 'God, what are you doing? You know these people need water. Why would you do this?' I remember being really upset and angry. And then I wondered: maybe four is enough. We sometimes want to be over-productive and are too task-orientated, but the local people were still praising God and doing all the things that they do. These are things that I still struggle with, and I've learned not to ask the 'whys' because it doesn't help.

6

Natural disasters or national disasters?

There are many different kinds of disasters in our world today. For one, the refugee crisis continues to loom large. Each year, thousands of families fleeing war and persecution risk their lives to cross the Mediterranean in little more than a dinghy. Not everyone makes it, and yet they tell us it is worth the risk. Some would rather die than return home, which begs a vital question: what horrors have they left behind to precipitate such desperate thinking? Killings, bombings, corruption, homelessness, looting, kidnapping, rape, domestic abuse, racial abuse, human trafficking – the list could go on. There are so many kinds of disasters today, so many of which are unfolding on a national scale. Whole countries are in chaos.

Some might be tempted to place these kinds of disasters in the same category as natural disasters. Yet it would be more accurate to call them 'national disasters' than 'natural' ones. Why? Because wars and refugee crises are rooted in and caused more by *moral evil* than *natural evil*, even though *natural evil can sometimes play a part*. In other words, they are caused more by people treating one another badly than by activity within the natural world. And so there are 'national disasters' driven by the actions of people, and then there are 'natural disasters' caused primarily by events in nature.

Yet, when it comes to disasters such as drought and famine, the situation is more complex. Both human and natural factors can play a role and even 'feed off' each other. Inclement weather can lead to drought, causing crops to fail. Or crops may be eaten by swarms of locusts or be incinerated by wildfires. In theory, thanks to engineering, no-one need be at the mercy of drought and famine. Irrigation systems and boreholes can compensate for unpredictable weather, and pesticides help to sustain a crop yield. But political instability and conflict can also prevent food and clean water from reaching those who need it, often precipitating national disasters.

In Mao's mid-twentieth-century China, upwards of 45 million people died of starvation as a result of his catastrophic policies. The ironically named 'Great Leap Forward' led to what is now known as 'the Great Famine' and was truly a national disaster. We should also remember the nineteenth-century Irish Potato Famine that arose from multiple crop failures due to potato blight, a disease caused by *Phytophthora infestans*. The failure of the British Government to help, under Prime Minister Lord John Russell, led to the loss of 1 million lives to starvation, typhus or other famine-related diseases. A further 2 million emigrated, mostly to the USA.

Famines have caused untold suffering for millennia. Until very recently, in most parts of the world, a long agonizing death by starvation lay only one or two harvests away for many people. However, historian Yuval Harari, in his book *Homo Deus*, argues that today the biggest threats to life – famine, plague and war – have been reined in and 'transformed from incomprehensible and uncontrollable forces of nature into manageable challenges'.[1] According to Harari, now that on the whole these biggest 'beasts' have been tamed and we are no longer living 'hand-to-mouth', or defending ourselves from tribal factions, we are enabled to have a more 'healthy, prosperous and harmonious' existence.[2] As a result, the human race has time to spare and will increasingly be able to redirect its efforts to other things. Harari writes well and his thesis has some truth to it. And yet it sits in stark contrast to the reality of the COVID-19 pandemic, as well as the accounts of aid workers such as Becks, and military personnel, who might argue that war, famine and plague are far from solved.

But even if they were, it seems that in the Western world they have been replaced by the equally challenging problems of obesity, mental health decline, disease in the elderly, and rising cases of suicide especially among young people. Are these problems any less debilitating? Do we find ourselves in the 'healthy, prosperous and harmonious' world that Harari describes? Far from it. Like plucking out grey hairs from an ageing head, we try to eliminate one problem and find that two more surface in its place. Is this just the way the world is, or are there deeper explanations to which we can appeal?

Becks' story reminds us that suffering churns up deep questions. Why would eleven out of fifteen boreholes be completely dry when people desperately need water? Why do wars, famines and plagues exist in the first place? Why do weather fronts combine to yield devastating storms *at all*? Why are there moulds such as *Phytophthora infestans* lurking in plant ecosystems that can gain the upper hand and cause potato blight? Why does cell division even have the capacity to spiral out of control, leading to a build-up of cancerous tissue? Why are there viruses that hijack and split open healthy cells, with power to bring humans and nations to a halt? Sociological, genetic and geophysical explanations bring us a long way in making sense of these things and are to be welcomed. But are they enough for a complete understanding of the world in which we find ourselves?

Birth pains

The Christian faith has something to say at this point. Although there are forces of nature that can sustain life and cause death, this is not the whole explanation. It isn't sufficient to say that this is simply the way the world is. Somehow, there are also destructive forces that are woven into the physical world, into our very biology and into the human heart. The natural world and our bodies are beautiful and able to be strong and do incredible things, but there is also brokenness.

There are two different ways in which the 'world' is referred to in the New Testament: *ktisis* and *kosmos*. *Ktisis* signifies God's creative handiwork whereas *kosmos* denotes powers or forces that enslave the created order and throw it into chaos. Both of these dimensions are at play. In his letter to the church in Rome, the apostle Paul describes the natural world as being in a state of frustration and transition:

> For the creation was subjected to frustration, not by its own choice, but by the will of the one who subjected it, in hope that the creation [*ktisis*] itself will be liberated from its bondage to decay and brought into the freedom and glory of the children of God.
>
> We know that the whole creation has been groaning as in the pains of childbirth right up to the present time.[3]

These words point out that the natural order is not at peace with itself, but is frustrated, writhing and groaning, similar to a woman in labour. This might seem like a strange way to describe the forests, mountains and coastlines that we retreat to for their tranquillity, and as I look out of my window on an English late spring day, the only 'noise' from nature to be heard is the sound of rain. What exactly is meant by this 'groaning'?

Well, a woman in labour is not in a finished state. She is about to produce another human being. A woman in labour is in a state of transition. There is more to come, and the pain won't stop until delivery is complete. And according to the biblical view, the same is true of the natural world. The world around us is not yet finished, and the pains, creaks and groans that sometimes emanate from the natural world are a reflection of this incompleteness. Our world is in transition. There is still more to come, and the pain won't stop until everything is put right. The very end of the Bible speaks not so much of 'heaven' but of a 'new heaven and new earth' in which God will make everything new.[4] But at the moment, we see frustration and transition.

What is the cause of this frustrated state of groaning? One view held by Christians is that this physical brokenness has a *spiritual cause*. The natural world is in a state of enslavement or 'bondage to decay' and 'subjected to frustration, not by its own choice, but by the will of the one who subjected it'.[5] Well, who is the one who subjected it? Right at the beginning of the biblical narrative the earliest humans, Adam and Eve, enjoy an unhindered relationship with God, with each other and with their natural habitat. Yet the Genesis account is clear that they are not alone in Eden. They are accompanied by a serpent who is said to be 'more crafty than any of the wild animals the LORD God had made'.[6] Many hours have been taken up discussing how these verses should be read, but they certainly need not contradict scientific and anthropological narratives. The serpent is seen as representing Satan, a being who enticed humans to turn away from God and become estranged from their maker. Christians refer to this event as 'the fall'.

Broken planet

What are the different ways in which thinkers have tried to explain the spiritual roots of nature's brokenness?

One view is the 'natural law view' expressed by philosopher Richard Swinburne.[7] According to this view, natural evils have been incorporated into the structure of the world by God right from the beginning, and they are necessary for allowing human free choice. For people to have genuine free will, their context needs to be operating according to stable and predictable laws of nature. Without these regularities, free will becomes impossible. For example, imagine I am choosing whether or not to drink a glass of water. The forces and impulses operating in my muscles will enable me to pick up the glass if I want to. The force of gravity will enable the water to flow into my mouth when the glass is tilted. Because of these regularities, the choice remains mine as to whether I drink the water or not. If the glass was sometimes impossibly heavy to lift, or sometimes flew out of my hand, then I would not be in a position to exercise choice in drinking the water. The 'natural law view' states that stable laws of nature are needed to enable human free will, but the flip side of those laws is that they can also have harmful effects. The H_2O in the glass is the same water that drowns in a tsunami or flood. Proponents of this view face the challenge as to why God couldn't have secured free will with different natural laws – laws that are equally stable but don't yield disasters and diseases.

Perhaps the best-known view is the traditional Augustinian view that natural evil is the result of a human fall. The natural world has been subjected to frustration and decay because of the actions of early humans and has been dragged along into this momentous act of rebellion by people against God. The consequences begin to be described by the Lord to the woman, that her pains in childbirth will greatly increase,[8] and to the man, that the very ground itself will be subject to a curse, making it unpredictable and hard to work with.[9] The 'human fall view' traces the arrival of disasters and diseases back to this point, although some may see the fall as worsening natural evils that were already present rather than precipitating them. Advocates of this view today include philosophers such as Stephen Webb[10] and William Dembski.[11] The 'human fall view' faces the challenge of how to make sense of the geological record that documents natural events, such as earthquakes and volcanic eruptions, as vastly predating the arrival of humans.

A third view, the 'pre-human fall view', links natural evil to an angelic fall that predates the fall of humans. This view states that God created not only humans but also angels, and just as there was a rebellion on earth, so there was also an earlier revolt in heaven – both the result of creaturely beings exercising their free will. Fallen angels plummeted to earth at an early stage in earth's history and destructive forces of evil have been at work in the natural world and in human biology ever since – certainly, since long before humans ever arrived. The 'angelic fall view' helps greatly in making sense of the geological record and of evolutionary accounts, but it faces challenges around why God would allow these destructive forces, responsible for vast animal suffering and death, to play such a pivotal part in a creative process that is seemingly deemed 'good' in Genesis 1. We will come to this question shortly. Advocates include theologians Michael Lloyd[12] and Greg Boyd.[13] An angelic fall is not inconsistent with the view that links the origins of evil to the fall of an angelic being, Satan.[14] There is every possibility that forces of evil have been at work in the natural world for a long time. In the Genesis account, the serpent is already present in Eden alongside the man and woman. The narrative leaves it open as to how long he has been there and the extent of the damage already caused.

Whatever the particular position taken, be it the 'natural law', 'human fall' or 'pre-human fall' view, the foundations are the same. Nature's brokenness cannot be explained merely in natural terms. There are also spiritual reasons for disasters and diseases.

Overly dramatic?

Chalking the world's problems down to a 'spiritual fall', be it of angels or people, may strike some as odd. David Bentley Hart puts it well:

Perhaps no doctrine strikes non-Christians as more insufferably fabulous than the claim that we exist in the long melancholy aftermath of a primordial catastrophe . . . [and] that the universe languishes in bondage to the 'powers' and 'principalities' of this age, which never cease in their enmity toward the kingdom of God.[15]

Yet, in seeking to resolve matters of emotional, psychological and physical distress, identifying root causes is vital if we are to heal. So could this also be true of spiritual matters? If there are spiritual root causes, then no amount of human progress will deliver the harmonious existence that Harari spoke of. We don't live in a merely physical world of natural laws, cause and effect, evolutionary adaptation and technological advances. There is also a deep brokenness, woven into the very fabric of our existence, that has a spiritual cause. There are forces of evil that are at work in nature, in biology and in every human heart. The natural world is beautiful but broken. The human body is beautiful but broken. People are beautiful but broken. The 'world' comprises *ktisis* and *kosmos*.

I imagine that few humanitarian aid workers need convincing of this reality as they pick up the pieces of people's lives that have been devastated by conflict, kidnappings, rigged elections, hunger and preventable diseases. But none of us is exempt. It was Russian historian, novelist and philosopher Aleksandr Solzhenitsyn (1918–2008) who, having experienced the horrors of Stalin's regime and brutal exile in Siberia, said that 'the line separating good and evil passes not through states, nor between classes, nor between political parties either – but right through every human heart – and through all human hearts'.[16]

According to the Christian faith, there is something beautiful yet broken about all of us. And we all experience the frustration and groaning of hurricanes and wildfires, of cancers and viruses, of wars and famine. We suffer, and at times may even contribute to, the pain of natural disasters and national disasters.

Pain and death in Eden?

Oxford is thought to have had a thriving dinosaur community, and on many occasions I have visited the Museum of Natural History with my children, to admire the skeleton models in the main hall. The Jurassic Coast from Devon to Dorset is also home to fossilized footprints of these beautiful yet terrifying creatures that once walked the earth. As people, we are avid consumers of crude oil and its by-products, made by the crushing of organic life forms over millions of years. If we are to accept the geological record, then how do we reconcile the reality that creatures of all kinds have been living, dying and fossilizing for many millions of years in the supposedly 'good' world that God made, long before humans arrived at the geological eleventh hour? During that time, new species emerged while others became extinct. Has God woven animal suffering and death into his process of creation, and if so, what does that say about him? Or are there different ways of thinking about this?

Christians hold different positions on the origins and place of death in the creation narrative. Some would say creaturely death is a necessary part of the evolutionary process;[17] others would say it is part of the problem.[18] Still others would argue that multiple factors are at play.[19] However, we don't need to look far into the Genesis 1 account to see that a world that is 'good' is not necessarily devoid of all forms of death. In Genesis 1:11–13 we read,

Then God said, 'Let the land produce vegetation: seed-bearing plants and trees on the land that bear fruit with seed in it, according to their various kinds.' And it was so. The land produced vegetation: plants bearing seed according to their kinds and trees bearing fruit with seed in it according to their kinds. And God saw that it was good. And there was evening, and there was morning – the third day.

Seed-bearing plants, trees and fruit are integral parts of the created world and seen as good by God. Yet death is a necessary part of their life cycle.

Plant and animal death

My husband and I are not natural gardeners, and it is rare for a plant to thrive under our care. Sunflowers, however, seem robust enough to hold their ground. During the 2020 pandemic, I became fascinated with this process, and in particular, the way that the one seed we planted not only became a flower that outgrew all of us in height, but also, by the end of its life, had produced dozens of new seeds, each one capable of becoming a giant flower. Plant death is itself a means of generating life and is implicit in Genesis 1. Jesus also mentions this process to illustrate how his own death will bring life to others: 'Very truly I tell you, unless a grain of wheat falls to the ground and dies, it remains only a single seed. But if it dies, it produces many seeds.'[20]

Some would also hold that God's creative process does not preclude the possibility of animal death. In his letter to the Roman church, the apostle Paul writes that 'sin entered the world through one man, and death through sin, and in this way death came to *all people*, because all sinned' (my emphasis).[21] In other words, human rebellion against God has introduced death to *people*, but not necessarily to *all living creatures*. Some theologians such as Christopher Southgate and scientists such as Denis Alexander[22] have taken this verse and others to suggest that plant and animal death was part of God's creative process and is part of the natural way of things. The instinct to kill for food is merely each animal playing its part in the diverse network of food chains and ecosystems and does not break a moral code in the same way that murder does. And, as Southgate highlights, even the asteroid impact that rendered dinosaurs extinct was that which enabled the rise of mammals and eventually sentient human beings.[23]

Further on in the text, it is implicit that Adam and Eve had some understanding of death, because of the words of the Lord to them: 'You are free to eat from any tree in the garden; but you must not eat from the tree of the knowledge of good and evil, for when you eat from it you will certainly die.'[24] If they had had no concept of death, this prohibition would have been meaningless, but Adam and Eve's future actions suggest that they did understand what was being said.

Positive pain

There is also reason to believe that some forms of physical pain already existed in this 'unfallen' world. After eating the forbidden fruit, Eve is told that her pains in childbearing will become 'very severe',[25] implying that there was some pain to begin with, only now it would be worse. A 'good' world with physical pain might seem counter-intuitive, yet a number of studies show that moderate physical pain can have a beneficial role in preserving life and is even essential to well-being.[26] Pain is the means by which we sense our environment, and our pain receptors alert us to problems. When this sense is impaired or absent, for example in conditions such as leprosy, life expectancy and quality of life are vastly lowered. So, as we dig a little below the surface, we see that not all forms of pain and death are necessarily bad and that the question of what a 'good' and unfallen world may have looked like is far from straightforward.

What can we say about the character of God in the light of the world he has made and the way he may have made it? It's important to point out that linking all creaturely pain and death to a traditional human fall does not dissolve the moral dilemma either. Why should the whole animal kingdom begin to suffer purely as a result of human action? Is that not also unjust? Either way there are concerns, as mentioned earlier. Yet if some forms of pain and death are woven into the creation process, it is because these processes are inherently life-giving, not because God is sadistic and delights in inflicting pain and suffering on innocent creatures.

Wolves and lambs

But even this may not constitute the whole story. The prophet Isaiah predicts that one day in the future, Jesus will return and will make everything on earth new, and this will have an impact on all of creation, including animals and how they relate. Glimpses of this new era, even though they have been interpreted in many different ways, say extraordinary things:

> The wolf will live with the lamb,
>   the leopard will lie down with the goat,
> the calf and the lion and the yearling together;
>   and a little child will lead them.
> The cow will feed with the bear,
>   their young will lie down together,
>   and the lion will eat straw like the ox.
> The infant will play near the cobra's den,
>   and the young child will put its hand into
>   the viper's nest.
> They will neither harm nor destroy
>   on all my holy mountain,
> for the earth will be filled with the knowledge
>   of the LORD
>   as the waters cover the sea.[27]

A time is coming when God will bring about a great reconciliation – a time when the kingdom of heaven is fully seen and lived out, and when the Lord will be known throughout the earth. The benefits will fill every aspect of the created world, even down to animal relations. The strong will no longer prey on the weak. There will no longer be competition for survival nor predation. Children will no longer be at risk around wild animals. It is hard to imagine such a world, but it's not wrong to long for the 'harmonious' world that Harari spoke of. If it's true that creation 'waits in eager expectation' for new things,[28] perhaps here we have a glimpse of what these things could be?

Can the brokenness be fixed?

After the 2004 tsunami, whole villages were grieving; everybody had lost somebody. Where do people take their pain and trauma in a situation like this? No-one is in a fit state to bear the grief of another. They have plenty of their own grief to contend with. In John's story of the tsunami back in chapter 1 we learned that 'what they needed was someone from the outside to come in and just listen', someone who wasn't consumed by personal grief and would therefore have the capacity to carry the burdens of another. We learned of the comfort that the translators brought by doing exactly that.

In a similar way, God longs to come alongside us and sit with us in our trauma and pain and listen. God has not simply left us to fend for ourselves in this broken world. He has entered it as Jesus Christ. When everyone around us is hurting and there is no-one to turn to, there is Jesus, the one who is not wracked by his own personal grief and therefore is able to bear ours. Jesus was described by one of the writers of the Psalms hundreds of years earlier in this way:

The LORD is close to the broken-hearted
    and saves those who are crushed in spirit.[29]

Some might say that Christians wheel God out to make us all feel better about ourselves, as a kind of 'crutch' to get through tough times. This view, initially voiced by twentieth-century psychologist Sigmund Freud (1856–1939), has been used by many to debunk Christianity. The flaw that some fail to see is that the same thinking can also be used to debunk atheism. How do we know that atheism isn't also a crutch deployed by those who cannot cope with the prospect of answering to a higher being at the end of life? Freud's 'crutch' can be used to argue for or against God and doesn't really help to move the conversation along. Something that does move the conversation along is to establish whether or not we agree that the world is broken. I won't have been able to persuade all readers, of course. But for those in agreement, would we also agree that the solution to a broken world is something or someone who isn't broken? Something or someone who understands the brokenness but isn't part of it?

Several years ago, my son, Ethan, was pushed off a climbing frame and injured his ankle. We ended up in hospital and found that, being unable to put weight on that ankle, he needed crutches – in fact they were crucial to his recovery. Crutches help to heal a broken bone because crutches – to state the obvious – are not broken and can be pulled in close to our body, enabling us to lean fully on them for support. In our broken world, what if there was someone who was close enough to lean on, but who was not broken like us and therefore able to bear the full weight of this earth's fractures and rifts – biological, geological, relational, emotional? If that kind of being exists, then there is hope for mending our broken world. There is a way through despair, depression, illness, famine, national disasters and natural disasters. There is a way to walk again, even in the face of deep tragedy.

The Christian faith says this being exists. God entered human history as Jesus Christ. Jesus came close to the broken-hearted. He healed diseases, calmed storms, raised the dead. He came head to head with the brokenness and evil in nature, in biology and in people. Jesus did not just walk away from hurting people, or wring his hands in resignation; he looked hurting people in the eye and did something about their suffering. Jesus also claimed to be able to satisfy the deepest longings that people have – spiritual longings that go far beyond physical hunger and thirst. He said, 'I am the bread of life. Whoever comes to me will never go hungry, and whoever believes in me will never be thirsty.'[30]

Easter earthquakes

I remember going to see Mel Gibson's *The Passion of the Christ* at the cinema when it was released in 2004. There was something very surreal about sitting in the cinema in stunned silence at the end thinking that there was surely no greater and more crucial event in history than this. The brutal death of a perfect man for a world that couldn't care less. And then his rising from the grave. But moments later we were walking out through a shopping mall having our senses bombarded with fashion ideas, the aroma of popcorn and the latest chart-topping songs. I couldn't find a way to reconcile these two experiences. It would have been so easy to simply let the mall hold sway and forget about what I had just seen. But I needed to get home and be somewhere quiet.

On that first Easter, Jesus endured betrayal, abandonment, mockery, beatings, flogging, injustice, and deep psychological, emotional and spiritual anguish. Finally, he stared down the ultimate enemy, death itself, and it is here that we see another connection between the spiritual and physical worlds. The death and resurrection of Jesus, arguably the two most spiritually significant events in history, were both accompanied by earthquakes. In the moment when Jesus breathed his last we read that 'the curtain of the temple was torn in two from top to bottom. The earth shook, the rocks split and the tombs broke open. The bodies of many holy people who had died were raised to life.'[31] We then read what happened two days later:

> After the Sabbath, at dawn on the first day of the week, Mary Magdalene and the other Mary went to look at the tomb.
>   There was a violent earthquake, for an angel of the Lord came down from heaven and, going to the tomb, rolled back the stone and sat on it.[32]

Once again, these descriptions may seem far-fetched to some. But they speak of a close correspondence between natural events and spiritual events. We also know that the whole known area became dark at the moment of Jesus' death, to the extent that even non-Christian sources such as the Jewish historian Josephus made note of it. Were these events in the natural world a marker of the magnitude of what had just happened? Of the literally earth-shattering impact of Jesus' death? Were they indicating the far-reaching effects of what Jesus came to do?

So what exactly did Jesus come to do? He came to usher in the kingdom of God on earth, in all of its beauty and goodness. He came to reconcile people to God, by bearing the weight of their internal brokenness, known as sin, and extending forgiveness to us all. The catastrophic effects of national disasters are prevented one person at a time, and begin with each person asking the question: *What is my response to the person of Jesus Christ?*

Locusts, Ethiopia 2019–20

Mesfin, Tearfund Programme Development and Communications Lead

I've been in Addis Ababa for the last three and a half years working first in humanitarian and emergency response, and more recently in development programmes and communication throughout Ethiopia. A key part of my work has been to respond to locust infestations in both northern and southern parts of the country.

It's normal for us to have locust swarms, but the infestations of 2019 and 2020 were of a kind we've never experienced before, in terms of the numbers of insects, the damage inflicted and the terror they sent out. At first, small numbers of locusts appeared. We didn't think anything of it, but with hindsight, they were a warning sign, a precursor to a much larger invasion.

In Ethiopia it is natural to expect sunlight throughout the day, and directly overhead, since we're near the equator. But the sky above our heads became dark within minutes. The sound of millions of insect wings vibrating was unlike anything we had heard before. A familiar sound would not have been so terrifying, and this one had a rhythm to it that became louder and louder. Desert locusts swept in, covering every possible piece of land. People reacted in different ways. Some weren't sure what was happening. Others were saying that this must be the end of the world.

There were so many locusts that the traditional ways of controlling a swarm, such as chasing them away, were useless. The numbers were beyond the capacity of the regional and even national government. For farmers, the timing was catastrophic: it was just before the crops were about to be harvested, and within a matter of days farmers found themselves empty-handed. Every green plant, whether crops or pastureland, had been eaten. We never expected that kind of damage to be inflicted. More than 300 million kilograms of cereals of different kinds were lost, especially maize, sorghum and wheat. In neighbouring Somalia, 61% of the pastureland was lost, meaning that 61% of the population would be affected in one way or another. Other countries, such as Yemen, Djibouti and Kenya, were also badly affected.

The ripple effects were far-reaching. Losing your crops meant losing your income, and being unable to feed your family or send your children to school. If your family, and especially your children, can't eat, they will be more vulnerable to health problems. Not only that, but if the pastureland is gone, there is nothing for the animals to eat, so they start dying. And this can cause all kinds of social tensions that reach as far as some resorting to marrying their daughters off earlier than usual, as a way of reducing the number of people to feed. Urban areas are also affected because they are dependent on rural areas for food. A locust infestation means that food supplies to urban areas diminish. When that happens, inflation goes up, and food becomes too expensive for urban dwellers. The whole country suffers the impact.

If you know locusts are coming, there are things that can be done, given enough time. First, timely communication between different areas – regional sharing of information – would have helped us prepare. If the authorities in Yemen, Djibouti, Somalia or Kenya had warned us, we might have been able to save the crops. But of course, some of these countries, as is typical for the Horn of Africa, have many competing priorities in terms of security and stability. Yemen, for example, is already experiencing famine and civil war and has no stable government. Pestilence may be further down their list of priorities.

Second, in terms of preventative measures, drones could have been used to survey desert areas for approaching swarms, and they could be something to deploy in the future. Third, we could have harvested the crops earlier or used helicopters to spray them with pesticides. But in 2019 and 2020, by the time the helicopters arrived, we had already lost everything.

In the past, locust swarms were much smaller, more predictable and therefore manageable. They were part of the yearly cycle. But vast infestations on the scale of millions have arisen since weather conditions have become more extreme and unpredictable. We have been experiencing a lot more heavy rainfall and warmer temperatures, which provide ideal breeding conditions for locusts. The rain also causes rapid growth in vegetation, meaning that locusts are attracted away from the desert towards the crop-bearing pasturelands for food, where they cause destruction on a scale never seen before.

Global warming, desertification and deforestation are all playing a part. The east and south-east parts of the country are desert. If we do nothing, these arid areas will expand and claim new territory, each year edging closer and closer to the pasturelands in the highlands. Locusts breed in the desert, which means that as desertification takes effect, the multiplying locusts move closer and closer to a food source, making pasturelands and their crops increasingly vulnerable to infestation.

Desertification and deforestation happen when you have a rapidly growing population. Unless alternative job opportunities are created, people turn to farming. They move to the marginal areas, cut or burn down trees, and convert forest into farmland, to grow wheat and vegetables. Or they may produce charcoal, which also requires the cutting of trees. People in nomadic areas also fell trees to create pastureland to grow grass for their animals. Political instability in Ethiopia makes everything worse. A lack of jobs in urban areas forces even more people into rural areas, placing increasing strain on the land. Once deforestation has taken place, the land is vulnerable to erosion through winds or flash flooding, gradually turning a previously forested area into desert.

The speed of recovery all depends on how much support is being given either by the Government or by aid agencies. If help is given to replace lost animals and replant the pastureland, then recovery is possible within months. Without support it may take years to recover. Training could be provided to show communities how to build up a resilience that makes future recovery more likely. We see that communities with a diverse range of income sources are more likely to bounce back, whereas communities that focus on a single animal or crop are hit harder in the wake of an infestation.

Tearfund in Ethiopia is trying to help communities to recover and rebuild, despite the challenges of funding shortages and a small team. In the northern parts of the country we were able to help communities with a grant that we received from the Scottish Government. One person commented that, 'when everything turned ugly, God turned up through Tearfund to lift us up from this destitute situation'. They never expected help and support of this kind to come along and believed that God had sent people to their aid. When disaster strikes, people are affected in all kinds of ways, but we want to show them that there is always hope and a future.

7

What about insects that devastate?

In 2020, East Africa suffered its worst infestation of locusts for decades.[1] With the infestation only just shy of the category of 'plague', Kenya had not seen anything like this for seventy years, Ethiopia and Somalia for twenty-five years, and countries such as Yemen, Iran, Qatar, India and Pakistan were also inundated. These voracious insects are able to eat their own body weight in food each day. Swarms numbering as many as 70 billion, enough to cover New York City more than once,[2] can in just a few days destroy crops that would have fed thousands of people for a whole year.[3] For countries that already suffer food shortages due to war, famine and poverty, the devastation caused by pestilence makes life even harder, and 1 in 10 people on earth are affected.[4] Why is it that there are insects that raze areas of beauty and see to it that people go hungry? Why are there some seemingly pernicious corners of the natural world? Why would God create insects that cause devastation?

In chapter 1 we discussed part of actor and atheist Stephen Fry's response to Gay Byrne when he asked what he would say to God if it turned out to be true that God existed, and he found himself at the 'pearly gates'. In that part of his response, he questioned why God would allow bone cancer in children. Fry then continues by addressing another kind of childhood suffering:

Yes, the world is very splendid, but it also has in it insects whose whole life cycle is to burrow into the eyes of children and make them blind. They eat outwards from the eyes. Why? Why did you do that? You could easily have made a creation where that didn't exist. It is simply not acceptable.[5]

Fry probably has in mind the 2008 interview of Sir David Attenborough with broadcaster and TV presenter Jeremy Paxman in which he explains why he sees no need to mention God in his natural history programmes, no matter how beautiful the creatures at hand may be:

They always mean beautiful things like hummingbirds. I always reply by saying that I think of a little child in east Africa with a worm burrowing through his eyeball. The worm cannot live in any other way, except by burrowing through eyeballs. I find that hard to reconcile with the notion of a divine and benevolent creator.[6]

At first it was thought that the worm Attenborough was referring to was the *Loa loa*, a parasitic worm found in swamps and rainforests and common to West and Central Africa.[7] The more likely candidate, however, is the *Onchocerca volvulus*, a parasitic worm known to cause 'river blindness' or onchocerciasis. The disease is transmitted to humans by repeated blackfly bites which release microfilariae that burrow into the skin and organs, producing toxins. Symptoms include disfiguring skin conditions, severe itching and loss of sight which can lead to permanent blindness. More than 99% of infected people live on the African continent, and a study of cases in

2017 estimated there were around 220 million infected people, of whom 1.15 million suffered vision loss.[8]

When faced with these kinds of facts, many would share Attenborough's difficulties in reconciling eyeball-eating parasites with the notion of a loving God – especially when what is at stake is the sight of a child under eight years old. The atheism of Fry and Attenborough seeks to make sense of nature's beauty and brutality in a consistent way. What do they conclude? That neither the highs nor the lows of nature are reconcilable with notions of God; they are merely the product of natural processes. Bone cancer arises from harmful genetic mutations, which in a human population of 7 billion, and with each person carrying hundreds of billions of genes, are going to happen every so often. Worms burrow away because they are hardwired to eat whatever is in front of them, not because they desire to inflict blindness. They have adapted and evolved to survive, and the 'fittest' will prevail. According to the atheist worldview, cancer and the actions of the worm are neither right nor wrong. They just are.

Of course, this approach solves the problem at an intellectual level, but it doesn't resolve the fact that the suffering of children always feels wrong and *just should not be*. In chapter 1, we discussed how our inherent moral sense could be seen as a sign that we live in a moral universe made by a moral being known as God. The same arguments are helpful here.

In chapter 6, we discussed how there really is no such thing as a purely 'natural' disaster. The forces of nature and the actions (or inactions) of people are usually intertwined. In addition, we saw how the mechanisms that generate disasters are often also used to sustain life. Are these arguments helpful as we discuss pestilence?

Poverty

There are no easy answers when it comes to Fry's pathogenic nematode which, ecologically speaking, and to the best of our current knowledge, appears to do little to no good but plenty of harm. However, the role that poverty has in our vulnerability to natural disasters – now in this case in the form of disease – resurfaces here. Onchocerciasis can be prevented by spraying with insecticides that are readily accessible in wealthier countries, but less available and affordable in poorer ones. Even clothing to cover exposed skin is not a given in affected countries. Simple things that we take for granted when visiting as tourists are beyond the reach of local people.

A recent survey by the World Health Organization revealed that, in low-income countries, some of the biggest killers still include malaria, tuberculosis, diarrhoeal diseases and complications in childbirth, all of which are preventable with anti-malarials, vaccinations, clean water and midwifery, respectively.[9] Melinda Gates, in her book *The Moment of Lift*, describes the process of having her eyes opened to the vast differences between rich and poor in terms of their vulnerability to disease, especially in children. It was this process that led to the establishment of the Bill & Melinda Gates Foundation:

One researcher at [a] dinner told us about the huge number of children in poor countries who were dying from diarrhea and how oral rehydration salts could save their lives. Sometime after that, a colleague suggested we read World Development Report 1993. It showed that a huge number of deaths could be prevented with low-cost interventions, but the interventions weren't getting to people. Nobody felt it was their assignment. Then Bill and I read a heart-breaking article by Nicholas Kristof in *The New York Times* about diarrhea causing millions of childhood deaths in developing countries. Everything we heard and read had the same theme: Children in poor countries were dying from conditions that no kids died from in the United States.[10]

Although numbers of deaths are falling all the time and big improvements have been made in recent decades, there is still a long way to go to ensure that those in low-income countries are no longer vulnerable to illnesses that are preventable. Drug companies could do more to bring their priorities in line with world needs. Vaccine programmes must continue to be rolled out. Poverty undoubtedly makes people more vulnerable to disease, and insect-borne diseases are no exception. It isn't sufficient to simply point the finger at God. The responsibility for lifting people out of poverty and making health care accessible to those who most need it continues to rest with people.

Cumulative disasters

When we think about locust swarms, these have always been a predictable part of a yearly cycle; the problem is that vastly higher numbers of locusts have begun to descend, and in an unpredictable fashion. Why might that be? Here we see not only the role of human and natural factors, but also the cumulative effect of multiple kinds of natural disasters. Countless cyclones in 2019 and 2020 provided increased humidity and thus ideal locust breeding conditions. The higher incidence of cyclones and hurricanes is itself a consequence of rising temperatures on earth, which is increasingly seen as being driven by human activity. Swarms find it easier to breed and migrate when forests are cut back and desert areas expand in size. Deforestation can be exploitative but is often necessary to house and support growing numbers of people who can't find work in urban areas and so move to rural areas to take up farming. Lack of rain leads to drought. Erosion gradually turns farmland into desert – a migratory highway for locusts.

In summary, increased cyclones, rising air temperatures, deforestation and drought have all coalesced and contributed to the locust infestations of recent years.

The purpose of pests

Are there any benefits to pestilence? A classic question that children have asked in Sunday school – and an extremely valid one at that – is, 'Why did God make wasps?' Many a summer picnic has been disturbed by these black-and-yellow-striped pests that appear to serve no obvious purpose other than to threaten to sting us while we eat sandwiches in the park. Surely we would be better off without them? Apparently not. It appears that wasps play a vital role in ecosystems. An article by the Natural History Museum comments that

> without wasps, the world could be overrun with spiders and insects. Each summer, social wasps in the UK capture an estimated 14 million kilogrammes of insect prey, such as caterpillars and greenfly. Perhaps we should be calling them a gardener's friend.[11]

Creatures that, at first glance, appear only to be a nuisance actually play a vital role in balancing ecosystems and food chains. Sometimes, the purpose of pests is understood only when we understand their wider context, and when we try to remove them.

People have attempted to meddle with certain species with disastrous consequences, because of a failure to appreciate the complexity and balance of creaturely life. For example, in China's 'Great Leap Forward' of 1958–62, Mao Zedong launched his 'Four Pests campaign' to eradicate rats, flies, mosquitoes and sparrows. One might understand a desire to be rid of disease-carrying vermin and insects, but the policy against sparrows was on the basis that they ate too much grain, thus depleting supplies intended for people. The population were given incentives to play their part in driving sparrows to the point of extinction: shaking nests from trees, shooting them in flight, and even preventing them from landing, which led to death by exhaustion. Hundreds of millions of birds were killed in a matter of months. The consequences were dire. Mao's attempt to be rid of pestilence seriously backfired when, the following year, towns and villages found themselves overrun by locusts that devoured crops and tipped the country into famine. It turns out that sparrows didn't just eat grain, they also kept locusts, and countless other insects, under control.

We might question why particular insects exist, and why God might allow them. Part of our response is that there are vast ecosystems and networks of food chains within the animal kingdom that we know very little about, and in which seemingly unwanted members play a vital part. Humans interfere with them at their peril.

Prevention and treatment

Just as people can be made vulnerable to disease through the action or inaction of other people, so they can also be helped and even cured through innovation and medication. A striking part of Mesfin's story is how simple strategies such as the use of drones and good communications between countries could save the crops from being devoured by locusts. What does this look like for the worm mentioned by Attenborough and Fry? River blindness can be treated and full blindness prevented using a drug known as ivermectin. This can be given to individuals, but also large-scale preventative strategies have been underway for decades through the spraying of vast areas every year for twelve to fifteen years. A report by the World Health Organization provided details of its success:

> Between 1974 and 2002, disease caused by onchocerciasis was brought under control in West Africa through the work of the Onchocerciasis Control Programme (OCP), using mainly the spraying of insecticides against blackfly larvae (vector control) by helicopters and airplanes. This was later supplemented by large-scale distribution of ivermectin since 1989.
>
> The OCP relieved 40 million people from infection, prevented blindness in 600 000 people, and ensured that 18 million children were born free from the threat of the disease and blindness. In addition, 25 million hectares of abandoned arable land were reclaimed for settlement and agricultural production, capable of feeding 17 million people annually.[12]

In 1995, the African Programme for Onchocerciasis Control (APOC) was launched with the goal of eliminating the disease from remaining endemic countries. By 2015, the transition to complete elimination was underway. WHO has also declared four countries to be completely free of river blindness – Colombia, Ecuador, Mexico and Guatemala. Innovative science and engineering have a key role in relieving human suffering, especially that caused by pestilence.

We don't fully understand why such a destructive pest as the *Loa loa* or *Onchocerca volvulus* worm exists, and the reasons God might have for allowing it. Yet we also see that human beings have an extraordinary capacity to eliminate the blindness it causes, and on a country-wide scale, through innovation and medical treatment. Why are we able to do this? What reasons are given by different belief groups? Do human rationality and creativity make most sense as accidental products of a non-rational universe, or as products of a universe that has been undergirded by a rational, creative being right from the start? Of course, whole books have been written about this argument.[13] My point here is that we cannot simply dismiss God on the basis of worms without also having a good explanation for why people are also able to entirely eliminate their harmful effects. Perhaps human ingenuity and creativity itself points to God's existence?

Where does this leave us on the question of God and pestilence? We've noted the impact of poverty on vulnerability to disease, the cumulative effect that multiple kinds of natural disasters can have, and the vital role that seemingly nuisance insects play in vast ecosystems – ecosystems that we really only partially understand. Human beings also have an extraordinary capacity and desire to relieve the suffering of others.

Arguably, the most persuasive explanation for the foundation of our ability to create, innovate and love our neighbour is God himself.

COVID-19 pandemic, UK 2020

Ben, Neuro Intensive Care Consultant

I've been a doctor for just under seventeen years and at the time of writing am a consultant and clinical director of the Neuro Intensive Care Unit at University Hospital Southampton. This unit looks after critically ill patients with brain- and spinal cord-related problems, providing the regional care for just under 4 million people. We have fifty-five critical care beds in Southampton but were told to expect to occupy 380 at the pandemic peak. What people didn't know was that, prior to COVID-19, we were already at 90–105% capacity.

I've never been in a tsunami, but this felt a bit like being on the beach watching the tide go out, knowing that something massive was coming. We'd heard about hospitals in China. We were hearing scary stories from doctors in Italy having a terrible time working out which patients to ventilate, knowing that those without it would probably die. We even heard that some critically ill patients were in corridors being ventilated by hand.

The three ICU directors decided that we needed to work together on this, so we began to formulate our 'surge plan'. We took a stock check of everything, including the number of ventilators and critical care staff in the hospital. We sent some patients home and cancelled all non-emergency surgery. The real issue wasn't space, but staff. Normally in ICU, the ratio of patients to nurses is 1:1, and for good reason. Being critically ill is like running a marathon every day: it puts a huge strain on the body. The patients are often so unstable that constant supervision and care are required. Our 'surge plan' needed to

132

reduce that ratio to 1:6 – one nurse to every six patients. The problem is, that's simply not sustainable.

We started taking ward nurses, theatre nurses and recovery nurses, and training them up in critical care over one or two days, giving them crash courses in how to look after very sick patients. Many were terrified. Ward patients don't have tubes down their throat or lines in their neck – they are largely able to look after themselves. Critical care, however, involves a completely different kind of medicine. We also had training sessions for consultants and trainees from non-critical care, taking them through the basics of how to manage a ventilated patient and troubleshoot.

Nationally, we had huge drug and equipment shortages. Medicine that was usually commonplace was suddenly in low supply. At one point, we were questioning whether or not we'd have enough oxygen, something we'd never had to consider before. In Western medicine, oxygen 'on tap' is simply part of the infrastructure. But if the predicted 'surge' did come then there was a chance we would run out, at which point all the ventilators could stop. It also became clear very quickly that there wasn't enough personal protective equipment, or PPE. There were several days when we had enough for the next twelve hours but beyond that had to come up with makeshift solutions, such as employing a local fabric shop to make PPE for us.

When patients with COVID-19 started to come in, the biggest challenge for us all on the team was that we were caring for people with a disease that we knew nothing about. We know and understand the progression of, say, pandemic influenza. But COVID-19 is a very unusual virus with fascinating and disturbing complications. We were a couple of weeks behind London with respect to the spread of the pandemic and were able to learn from their experiences. Yet we were also in the extraordinary situation of caring for someone during the day and reading the latest information on the illness at home in the evening.

In the preparation and peak I was working seventy to eighty hours a week. There were not many days off, and fitting in a Sabbath was a challenge. A typical clinical day would start at 7.30 am and run until around 8 pm, sometimes later. In between staff discussions around patient care and conversations with families, I would do a ward round two to three times a day. One could take up to three hours so I would be in and out of full PPE. However, the nurses were sometimes doing seven to eight hours continuously in full PPE. You have to wear it to fully understand what this was like. First there's the mask, then your own scrubs, then a gown, then a visor and hat. Some staff had pressure sores on their noses from masks that didn't fit properly. Instead they had to wear hoods over their heads that made them look like Minions from *Despicable Me*, providing a brief comedy moment. Communication was difficult, however, because these hoods whirred away noisily, and it was hard to hear what people were saying on the outside. We sometimes had to yell at one another just to be heard. If that wasn't enough, most were self-isolating from their families and dealing with a very new and concerning virus. It's been a big emotional struggle, with quite a lot of tears. But I've also been reminded of how amazing the team is and of how resilient we can all be.

I didn't feel that I was risking my life. It was right and proper for us to have the PPE because we were in a particularly high-risk unit. But we saw many staff members from non-critical care wards and care homes admitted to us. As reported in the media, these places were less well stocked with PPE. This sat very uncomfortably with me. One colleague, a hospital postman who was well known by us all, tragically died. His story has been reported in the news.

The hardest moments have been to do with decisions around the end of life, when someone has had all the treatment we are able to give but is not getting any better. At this stage, we would normally bring the family in to explain in-person and give them time with their loved one. But with COVID-19, families have sometimes felt too scared to come in, or they live too far away, or they've needed to self-isolate. We also needed to be very strict with family visits to protect the patients, the staff and the visitors.

There was one really tough situation where we had to explain to a patient's wife over the phone that we were looking to withdraw treatment from her husband. That's a really horrible way to break this kind of news. It should be done face to face, so that you can give a hug or hold the person's hand. In this case, the family weren't able to come in. We turned off the ventilator and turned the oxygen right down to just air. A nurse sat with him, holding his hand as he passed away. This was really hard to see and just felt so wrong. This is not how things should be. The impact stays with you. Yet at the same time, there was no space to process. We needed to keep going and look to the next patient.

Eventually, when we look back, we will view COVID-19 as a career-defining experience. A foundational moment, the last of which was the flu pandemic of 1918. It's interesting that people have been describing this as a pandemic of biblical proportions. I've had a couple of colleagues ask me how I square it all with my faith in God. My response? I say I'm able to reconcile the fact that God is here, that he's good and powerful, and yet pandemics happen.

Some colleagues and I have been praying all along that the Holy Spirit would course through the corridors and wards of this hospital and descend a peace that helps morale and helps people connect with God. We've been praying for physical and spiritual healing for patients on ventilators and for staff too. Amid the grimness of it all, we want to know that there is someone we can trust, who has this in hand, even when it seems as if the 'wheels are falling off the cart'. I have asked, 'God where are you in this?' but it's been reassuring to see that he's in every single moment. God is not absent in our most difficult times. He is never closer than he is now.

8

Why would God allow pandemics?

COVID-19 has turned the world upside down. Until recently, many in the West experienced natural disasters as onlookers. We watched them through our TV screens and YouTube channels, wondering what it would be like to be caught up in a catastrophe and to suffer in such a deep and profound way. Coronavirus has changed this. The pandemic that has swept the globe in recent years has brought the reality of natural disasters into our very homes. At the time of writing, almost 580 million people have been infected around the world and almost 6.5 million have died. Now we each have a story to tell of the impact of COVID-19 on our lives and on our nations. Loved ones were taken from us all too prematurely, economies ground to a halt, and people were isolated, unable to spend time together. At its worst, up to two-thirds of the world's population were in lockdown at any one time. Instead of racing around, we were left alone with our thoughts, potential symptoms and fears. And all because of a rogue bat in a live animal market in Wuhan, China, or a laboratory error of catastrophic proportions. But we may never know what really happened.

As we process what we've been through, all kinds of questions will emerge – questions to do with government handling, questions concerning scientific understanding, and some will have spiritual questions concerning the big picture. Why do harmful viruses such as COVID-19 exist? And how do they fit with the belief that God created a supposedly 'good' world? To properly consider the big picture, it's worth first asking: what actually are viruses, and how do they work? For this we need to delve into some cell biology, a topic close to my heart as I studied biochemistry at university.

Virology experts would tell us that viruses are microscopic bundles of DNA, or its precursor RNA, encased in a protein bag. Unable to survive alone, the only way for a virus to propagate is to invade a living 'host' organism and, one cell at a time, to hijack its replication machinery. Thousands of copies of the virus then burst out of the cell, destroying it completely. At this point, the body's immune system begins fighting back using impressively named killer T cells that essentially swallow up virus cells. Recovery or decline is determined by whichever side is winning the battle.

But why do such viruses exist, leading to global pandemics?

Just the way the world *is*?

Let's begin by using the same approach that we took back in chapter 1. It's worth thinking first about our options for making sense of global pandemics if God does *not* exist. If matter is all that there is, then who is to say that pandemics are not simply nature's way of shaking things up and slimming down population sizes? Taken to its logical conclusions, perhaps a naturalistic view ought to let nature take its course and allow the fittest to survive? But, of course, this would come across as fairly callous. The succumbing of the then UK Prime Minister Boris Johnson and US President Donald

Trump to the virus was a reminder that these bundles of DNA are no selectors of persons. They simply carry out the instructions encoded within, to invade cells and self-replicate, regardless of the occupation and importance of their hosts.

Moreover, probability can explain why deadly viruses occasionally evolve, since there are known to be 'more than a quadrillion quadrillion individual viruses'[1] floating around on Planet Earth, each with a unique genetic code. In the words of a recent *National Geographic* article, that's 'enough to assign one to every star in the universe 100 million times over'.[2] By chance alone, a particularly deadly strain is going to arise every once in a while.

We could also look to all kinds of natural explanations as to why some people get ill and others don't. The wonders of the human immune system cannot be ignored here, enabling the vast majority of the global population to fight off the virus. This fact can sometimes be forgotten in media reporting. Scientists also tell us that our susceptibility to disease may have a genetic element to it, coming from the DNA we inherit from our parents. We also know that 'cause and effect' has a part to play: quality of sleep, a healthy diet and physical fitness all boost the immune system, but if neglected leave us vulnerable to disease.

Many of these are helpful and elegant insights that aid our understanding and are crucial in informing a strategic response. But they don't speak to the hurting person. They don't speak to the parents whose thirteen-year-old son died alone in a London hospital and whose funeral they were unable to attend. Genetics, 'cause and effect' and probability don't speak to the nurses and doctors who are now utterly exhausted having cared round the clock for the sick. Making the call as to who got the ventilator and who didn't. Isolated from their families. Having risked their own lives. They don't speak to elderly people who spent day after day isolated and vulnerable, desperate for a hug from their children and grandchildren.

Scientific explanations get us so far, but they don't make sense of the roller coaster of emotions that people have experienced in navigating this global pandemic. They simply describe the way that biology *is*. Viral transmissions are biological events. As discussed in chapter 1, to use the language of disaster or 'dis-ease' is to imply that something is wrong, which in turn implies that things ought to be better than they are.

From *is* to *ought*

But this then raises further questions: how should things be? And who decides? Moreover, how can the forces of nature tell us how things *ought to be*? They simply tell us how things *are*. For example, immunologists frequently reminded us that if people consistently followed social-distancing instructions, then the probability of our catching and transmitting COVID-19 would go down. And the number of cases in the overall population would also fall. But this told us nothing whatsoever about whether or not we *ought* to follow social-distancing measures. The majority were compliant, but a minority were not. The discovery of illegal parties attended by UK Government members only highlighted that rule-setters were some of the worst rule-breakers, claiming a need to 'let off steam' while the rest of the country was locked down and many died alone in hospital beds. How things *are* and how they *ought to be* are two very different things. Scientific explanations cannot get us from one to the other.

If science alone cannot make sense of our rawness, anger and frustration in the face of pandemics, then surely we need to look to explanations that lie beyond the realm of science and nature? Where do we find the best explanations for our instincts and emotions that accompany disease, sickness and viral infections? The same approaches that we applied to geophysical catastrophes in chapter 1 are also relevant here. In a purely material universe, morally sentient beings are certainly possible but would be something of an anomaly arising from the non-moral forces of nature. But if God exists, then our instincts and emotions make sense because we find ourselves in a moral universe. If God exists, then we can affirm that there is much that is good in this world and in the human body, but there is also something deeply wrong. There are healthy cells that fight off infection, but there are also viruses that hijack and destroy. God is good, but evil also pervades human behaviour and human biology.

For many, a world in which there are pandemics is a world in which God cannot possibly exist. Yet, as we discussed in chapter 1, it's actually *if* God exists that we find the most persuasive grounds for making sense of hurt and pain in this world. Our anger, frustration, sadness, grief and trauma are not things to be ignored, suppressed or prayed away. They are justifiable and valid, and are pointers not away from God but towards him.

Vital viruses

Pandemics such as COVD-19 can give the impression that viruses are extremely bad news for human beings. But it's important for us to note at this point that the material at the core of a virus is the key to biological life. There are forty-six DNA molecules within each of nearly 40 trillion cells in your body, and each one contains the underlying 'code' needed to produce all the different parts of your body: nerves, bones, organs, blood vessels, muscles and so on. Without DNA and its ability to replicate there would be no life at all, whether plant, animal or human. The individual building blocks of a virus are not inherently harmful.

In fact, these microscopic DNA bundles are vital for life and only 1% are harmful to people. Tony Goldberg, epidemiologist at the University of Wisconsin–Madison, commented in 2020 that

if all viruses suddenly disappeared, the world would be a wonderful place for about a day and a half, and then we'd all die – that's the bottom line . . . All the essential things they do in the world far outweigh the bad things.[3]

Viruses keep ecosystems in equilibrium, preventing any individual bacterium from becoming too dominant and using up all the oxygen. They have a protective role in humans, helping the body fight off harmful microbes. Viral activity has also been harnessed for therapeutic means. Scientists insert 'good' genes into viruses and deliberately allow them to invade and multiply in a 'host'. This is the basis of some forms of genetic engineering and gene therapy. David Quammen, writing for *National Geographic*, summarized the importance of viruses in this way:

The fact is, we live in a world of viruses . . . The oceans alone may contain more viral particles than stars in the observable universe. Mammals may carry at least 320,000 different species of viruses. When you add the viruses infecting nonmammalian animals, plants, terrestrial bacteria, and every other possible host, the total comes to . . . lots . . . Many of those viruses bring adaptive benefits, not harms, to life on Earth, including human life . . . We couldn't continue without them . . . Genes co-opted from viruses contribute to the growth of embryos, regulate immune systems, resist cancer . . . Eliminate all viruses . . . and the immense biological diversity gracing our planet would collapse like a beautiful wooden house with every nail abruptly removed.[4]

The majority of viruses play a life-giving role in our world, and so their existence doesn't seem to be the problem per se. Something good and life-giving has turned and been used to destroy, but only in 1% of cases. Perhaps the bigger problem, similar to geophysical disasters, is that we have become vulnerable to them in all kinds of ways. Viral infections turn into disasters when loved ones become ill and die.

Is my illness a punishment from God?

Within two weeks of the announcement of the first UK lockdown in March 2020, coronavirus came to our household. It was Easter weekend – Good Friday in fact – when my husband, Conrad, began to show symptoms, thus beginning our two weeks of self-isolation as a family of four. Within a few days, my daughter, Abby, developed the same fatigue, coughing and breathlessness. We were housebound, dependent on food deliveries from neighbours and church family. The stories in the news left us asking many questions: *Will we all get this by virtue of being under the same roof? What if both parents are unwell at the same time? What if one or both of us need hospitalization?* In our case, it didn't come to this, and within nine days the symptoms began to ease. During our time of quarantine, I noticed how strange it felt to admit that we had COVID-19. Even amid a global pandemic that was infecting millions, there was a subtle sense of shame that we were contaminated when others around us seemed to be free of contagion. Of course, most people caught it eventually, but the initial shame was still real.

The question of punishment is never really very far away from our thoughts. Some refer to the principle of karma, the Eastern view that suffering in this life is caused by deeds committed in a previous life coming to bear on the present, often captured by the expression 'What goes around comes around'. Karma says that individuals are responsible for whatever life throws at them in the present and must work on themselves in the hope that the next life will be better. Others appeal to the Islamic view that suffering is the will of Allah and is not to be resisted but surrendered to, come what may, often expressed as 'inshallah' ('if God wills it'). How are we to deal with personal pain? Is it true that my suffering is in some way divine punishment?

Job: the suffering of the blameless

The Bible does not shy away from personal pain. Chronologically speaking, its first book is not Genesis but Job, and the first subject addressed in its pages is this most universal of human experiences: suffering. We are introduced to the story of a godly man named Job who was said to be 'blameless and upright; [who] feared God and shunned evil',[5] and yet who also suffered greatly.

We learn that, within a short period of time, Job suffers multiple catastrophes, losing his farming business and staff, and then all of his children, and, as if that wasn't enough, he himself becomes gravely ill with a degrading and isolating skin condition. The prevailing view at the time was that suffering comes to those who deserve it. Job is visited by three friends, Eliphaz, Bildad and Zophar, who deeply believe that their companion has brought this trauma upon himself and is being disciplined by God because of his sin. They arrive intending to bring comfort to their anguished friend, but in the end serve only to increase his suffering with their repeated calls for him to repent and acknowledge wrongdoing. For a grieving and traumatized man with a body covered in sores and oozing puss, it is a nightmare scenario. Job insists he is blameless, and most of the book is taken up with the argument that ensues. Towards the end of the book, God speaks to Eliphaz to set the record straight: 'I am angry with you and your two friends, because you have not spoken the truth about me, as my servant Job has.'[6]

This whole interaction is vitally important as we think about how we should interpret suffering today. If even the most devoted and undeserving followers of God can expect to see dark days, then this ought to instil a hesitancy in those who want to interpret personal suffering as divine punishment. At the very beginning of the book of Job, we are party to a conversation of a different kind. A conversation that Job himself can't see. A conversation between God the Creator and Satan, a fallen angel who is said to be 'roaming throughout the earth, going to and fro on it'[7] looking for lives with which to wreak havoc. There is so much that we don't understand, but, in general, we suffer not because of divine punishment, but because of the reality of evil at work in the world, impacting behaviour, biology and nature.

Jesus

If suffering was divine punishment, then we would have expected Jesus to affirm this, and yet he does the opposite. Jesus rubbed shoulders with people suffering all kinds of physical illness: people with leprosy, congenital blindness, paralysis, fever, chronic bleeding, seizures and severe pain. Yet Jesus did not treat them as though they were receiving their just deserts for past sins. Instead, he looked hurting people in the eye and did something about their suffering.

We are told that right at the beginning of Jesus' public life he 'went throughout Galilee, teaching in their synagogues, proclaiming the good news of the kingdom, and healing every disease and illness among the people'.[8] Those whom doctors had long given up on were restored and given new hope. People who were socially distanced due to contagion were reinstated in the community. Jesus was even able to step into grieving households and do the seemingly impossible, reversing the worst of all illnesses – death itself.

The notion of punishment simply does not square with Jesus' care and compassion for the sick. Suffering people mattered to Jesus, and he did not simply wring his hands or pronounce judgment. Instead, he intervened to bring healing and life. The afflicted were not being targeted by an angry God; they were experiencing the consequences of living in a broken world, in which everyone is caught up one way or another. It was precisely because every human life is precious and because disease and sickness are not divine punishment that Jesus opened his arms wide to people in pain. In doing so, he overturned the cultural norms of his day.

Today, we might be hesitant to ask God for help in our suffering because of a concern that it is God who has afflicted us in the first place. Perhaps we picture an angry, distant God – if we picture God at all. Or we presume that, given the many disasters around the world, God's hands are tied, and he is too busy with more important work. We have a terrible phrase in the West, that 'there's always someone worse off than you'. This may be true, and sometimes looking outwards can give us perspective on our own situation, but it does not mean our suffering is unimportant to God. At the start of his ministry, Jesus laid out his manifesto:

> The Spirit of the Lord is on me,
>   because he has anointed me
>   to proclaim good news to the poor.
> He has sent me to proclaim freedom for the prisoners
>   and recovery of sight for the blind,
> to set the oppressed free,
>   to proclaim the year of the Lord's favour.[9]

Jesus brought healing and transformation to people one person at a time. Individuals mattered. Every life is precious to him. You matter to God. Will you bring your suffering to him? As Ben put it, 'God is not absent in our most difficult times. He is never closer than he is now.'

Earthquake, Nicaragua 1972

Rosie, local resident

It was the evening of 23 December 1972. *Nochebuena*, Christmas Eve, was about to start. At around 10 o'clock, my husband was sitting working in the living room when there was a loud rumble, as if a big rock had crashed to the ground. We lived right in the middle of a seismic zone, and suspecting it wouldn't stop there he came into the bedroom to change his clothes. I was already almost asleep and so he didn't mention anything.

I'm told that just before it happened there was a deafening silence. Dogs everywhere started hiding. Animals know before we do. People were looking at them, realizing that something was about to happen, but not knowing exactly what. It was something that you could almost feel in the air.

When the earthquake struck, I was asleep, and I woke up to the walls moving and disintegrating around me. At first, I thought I was still asleep and dreaming because I wanted to open my eyes. But then I realized that my eyes were already open. I couldn't see because of falling dust and debris. It was really difficult to assimilate reality in that moment.

I knew there was a God – I used to like gazing at the sky, looking to nature and the stars, looking for him. I was raised with a strong Catholic faith, believing that there was a God – a Father, a Son and a Holy Spirit. Growing up, we would recite prayers at bedtime, supper time or when we were on our way out of the house. I knew Jesus was alive, but I didn't know him. Yet now, I was sure that if I cried out to him, he would hear me. It was an innocent faith in that moment, and I wasn't really questioning. There's a phrase in Spanish that's akin to saying, 'May the Holy Trinity protect me.' I got up from the bed and immediately began crying out and pleading the words 'the blood of Christ' and 'May the Holy Trinity protect me.' Those were the only simple phrases I had.

My daughter was in a crib, and the first thing I did was go to see if she was OK and take her in my arms. But my husband told me to leave her, that she was safer in the crib. It's a moment of great shock. You have no time to think. I waited for the earth to stabilize. After the first big shock had finished, I reached for my daughter. Her ears were completely filled with debris and dust. My husband said, 'The door.' We began to figure out a way to climb out of the house, grabbing whatever was left of the walls for something to hold on to. All you can think of is your life. You don't think of taking anything with you. The most valuable thing is life, but that's all we had. I looked into what had been the living room but found myself looking out into the street. There was dust everywhere, reflecting light from the street.

That was the last time I was in my home. I never went back. We made it out with the clothes on our back. Ultimately, the house collapsed. There might've been a chunk of wall left somewhere, but everything else was rubble. I never found out what happened to my neighbours, except that many people died.

On the streets, everyone was looking to the sky and kneeling and lifting their arms and asking for help. People were screaming and just crying out to God. The city was unrecognizable, as if it had been bombarded from the air, like in the middle of a war. The sound that I heard has been in my mind until this very day. I can still hear it. It was like a breath coming out from the earth.

Some people seemed to lose all reason. There was a man holding on to the bumper of a car during the aftershocks, saying, 'Hold on to the car, hold on to the car.' He kept yelling for people to come and hold on to the car as an anchor. I just stared at this man, thinking he was crazy.

Other people looked as if they had been stuck in quicksand and came out dripping in mud and worse. Again, I just stared at them, still not understanding what was happening. People were relieving themselves in the streets. People were panicking. I had put a blanket on my daughter's back, but a lady came by, got close to me and just took the blanket. I didn't say anything to her. It was difficult to think and react well. You lose your grasp on reality. I just stared at her.

I looked around and still thought it was a dream because there were fires everywhere. In that moment all I could do was lift up my eyes to the heavens and say, 'My God', because I didn't really know how to pray, except 'Help me.' We were right in the middle of the fires and needed to get out of the area.

Everyone was fleeing. Aftershocks kept coming. It seemed as if the earth was about to open up, and I was afraid that we wouldn't make it to safety. I walked for about a mile barefoot, in just a cotton nightgown, through sewage water, broken glass, excrement and vomit. Incredibly, I wasn't hurt at all, not even a single cut. I began to pray the Lord's Prayer as we walked, looking for an open space to spend the rest of the night. We arrived at an old military airfield and stayed until sunrise.

In the morning, we learned that everything in Managua had been destroyed. The buildings weren't prepared for a massive earthquake, and there were many deaths. Where I lived there was a neighbourhood that became nicknamed 'ghost town' because only one person came out alive. No-one ever forgot this one man emerging from nothing. The name still stands today. There's also a story of a nightclub in the centre from which no-one came out alive. The earthquake caught them dancing, and that's how they went.

In a catastrophe, you get to know people for the first time, even family members. Immediately after the earthquake, we went to some relatives to ask for help, but they turned us away. I don't know why – it might have been because they were assisting other family members and didn't have the means to help us. Instead it was friends who gave us shelter and food, and if it hadn't been for them, we wouldn't have made it.

We didn't receive any relief or government help, and learned afterwards that vast amounts of international aid came into the country but the citizens never received it. There was so much corruption that nothing ever reached the people. Scarcity, instability, hunger and thirst were a daily reality. We didn't know what to do or where to go. Hundreds of thousands of Nicaraguans were needlessly left to die while leaders pocketed money from the international community. This in part led to the revolution that began six years later, which was another time of great fear and of not knowing if I was going to survive from one moment to the next. I felt in my heart a great need to forgive, to ask for forgiveness, and to be right with God.

We finally left for the USA in 1984. The deep hunger in me continued, but I didn't know where to find what I was looking for. I worked long hours and would sit on the buses in San Francisco and say, 'Lord, what am I doing in this place? What am I doing here?' And I would look for anyone on the street who might have a Bible with them. I explored many possibilities, from the Jehovah's Witnesses to the Seventh-Day Adventists. I would go and study with them. I used to like walking by 24th Street and Mission because there were street preachers with megaphones. I would sit down and listen to them. Until I was finally invited to a Christian service. I think that, looking back, I was always ready. I walked into the church and heard the teaching. There was an invitation and I went up and received Christ. Like many when they receive Christ, an overwhelming peace entered my heart, and I felt very light, very joyful, very happy. Yes, there were difficulties that came along. But that's how I gave my life to Christ. It was 1989.

I was traumatized for several years after the earthquake. For a long time, I went to bed fully dressed, and I carried an emergency bag at all times. I couldn't walk into a house without inspecting it for structural soundness and checking for the nearest exit, and I was always ready to run outside at a moment's notice. There are things that stay with you for a long time. I was young, and this experience formed a big part of my character. I learned not to lean so much on material things, nor be so attached to my possessions. As the years went by, I learned to value life a lot more.

The ruins at the centre of Managua, the epicentre, are still there to this day. It's like a city without a face now. They didn't rebuild because the fault lines are so big. It's what's known as a seismic city. Today people navigate around the city based on the earthquake. There's old Managua, and new Managua. Old Managua is where it happened.

Being caught in the centre of a massive earthquake and becoming homeless overnight might cause some people to say that there must be no God. But I had survived with my life and with my family, and that was everything. Many had lost loved ones. I can't remember if I thanked God at the time, but I do remember feeling thankful later. It didn't cross my mind to say that God did not exist. Sometimes in difficult moments we might think that God has forgotten about us. But that's different from denying his existence.

9

Why doesn't God just intervene anyway?

There is no such thing as an entirely natural disaster. Throughout this book we have looked at the different ways in which natural factors and human factors intertwine, and how people have an important role to play in minimizing and preventing deaths. But this doesn't resolve the question why there should be any deaths at all. People do not assess or experience suffering simply by scale. A natural disaster that kills just one person calls for answers as much as one that claims the lives of many thousands. And if God exists, we can't escape the fact that he still appears to be the initiator. If one of my children was in danger and there was something I could do, I would try everything in my power to help. Why doesn't God do the same? Why does he intervene to prevent disaster in some cases but not in others? When it comes to disease and sickness, why do some receive healing from God whereas others don't?

Does God heal today?

When Jesus walked the earth, he began to talk a lot about the kingdom of heaven, saying that it had come near in ways that had never happened before. Accompanying these words were signs of this kingdom in the form of people being healed, reconciled and even raised from death. A new era was ushered in – the kingdom of heaven on earth, where death and decay were reversed and people were restored. Yet, at the same time, death and decay had not disappeared entirely. Not everyone alive at the time of Jesus was healed – the old way of things was still also part of life.

Theologically speaking, we live in a kind of 'in-between time' in which the kingdom of God has arrived, but death and decay are still with us. When we pray for healing for someone and that person is healed, it is another reminder that the kingdom of God has come near in Jesus, and that one day it will be fully established. It's a bit like how a warm spring day in the UK is a reminder that summer is coming. But when we pray for healing and it doesn't happen, this is not a sign of divine displeasure. If healing doesn't come, it is not because we didn't pray hard enough, or because we had insufficient faith, but it is a reminder that the kingdom of God is not yet fully established on earth. Sometimes we are healed, and sometimes we are given grace and strength to patiently endure. Either way, the love and presence of God are close at hand for each person. And we are encouraged to ask for healing and to leave the outcome to God. Nicky Gumbel, a former vicar and founder of *Alpha*, a course designed for people exploring the Christian faith,[1] comments that if we don't ask for healing, for sure no-one will be healed, but if we do ask, there is the possibility that some people will be healed.[2]

As for why some survive a natural disaster whereas others die, or why some are healed but others aren't – this is where we reach the limits of human understanding. There are no easy answers to this question, especially for those whose loved ones have died at the hands of nature's forces. But we can say this. The God whom Christians believe in has not let events spin out of control. He is not aghast and wringing his hands. God somehow remains sovereign even over events that are devastating and confusing to us. Every human life is precious to him. He sees a far bigger perspective than we do. Here and now, the risen Christ promises to never leave us, no matter how deep and dark the valley we have to walk through. He promises to comfort us in ways that the world cannot. There is strength we never knew was possible, and there is hope for another day because he is alive and with us. In Christ, for those who ask, our prayer for healing will ultimately be answered with a resounding 'yes'. A day will come when there will be complete restoration for everyone – a day when all things will be made new.

Modern medicine

Even if we don't see dramatic healing from God, one of the ways in which God does bring healing today is through the care we receive from nurses, doctors, counsellors, surgeons, psychologists and psychiatrists. Antibiotics, anaesthetics, therapies, vaccinations, painkillers, C-sections – these treatments and others have relieved suffering and saved lives.

We are indebted to those who work tirelessly in our hospitals, doctors' surgeries and care homes to play their part in curing the sick. At the height of the COVID-19 pandemic, all involved paid a high price, self-isolating in hotels and Airbnbs to prevent the spread of the virus, forfeiting the comfort and closeness of their families. Some paid the highest price of all and died as a result of helping others. In the UK, this sacrificial work was celebrated every Thursday evening as people stood on their doorsteps and offered several minutes of applause. To the modern mind, there is no question that those who are ill should be helped and their physicians held in high esteem. We instinctively affirm that helping the sick in this way is good and right.

Yet the mandate to care for the sick and vulnerable has not emerged from nowhere. It has its origins in the teaching and rationale of Judeo-Christian belief. The Graeco-Roman world into which the church was born took the view that disease and sickness were punishment from the gods for past mistakes. The afflicted were simply getting what they deserved and therefore did not warrant help from anyone. Nor would anyone want to risk catching whatever they had. The infirm were separated from the community and left to stew in their own misery. Even newborn babies with deformities and disorders, or who were simply born female, were abandoned and left to die in the open air.[3]

Love your neighbour

Christians, or 'Galileans', on the other hand, became known for befriending those whom society had rejected and for upholding the most important commandments to 'Love the Lord your God' and 'Love your neighbour as yourself.'[4] If all people are made by God and carry his divine imprint, then each person has intrinsic value and worth regardless of the condition of their body and status in society. Hospitality or charity to the sick was an inherently Christian practice. The first larger-scale hospital that came to be known was the Basileias established by Basil of Nyssa, bishop of Galatia, along with his sister Macrina in AD 369, and was home to people with all manner of disease and sickness. His motivation, in the words of historian Tom Holland, was that 'there was no human existence so wretched, none so despised or vulnerable, that it did not bear witness to the image of God. Divine love for the outcast and derelict demanded that mortals love them too.'[5]

This same approach was also what motivated Christians to care for the sick in times of epidemic in the ancient world. As Rodney Stark points out, Roman people who had the means simply fled the disease-ridden cities to 'cleaner' rural areas, removing themselves from harm's way.[6] In the second century, a particularly lethal fifteen-year-long plague, thought by some to have been the first occurrence of smallpox, wiped out between a quarter and a third of people in the Roman Empire. Even Emperor Marcus Aurelius eventually succumbed to the disease in AD 180. This epidemic was named the 'Plague of Galen' because it coincided with the lifetime of the famous Roman physician. Yet Galen, for all his knowledge of the human body and its ailments, had surprisingly little to say about this plague. He too had headed for the hills. The Christians, in contrast, remained in the cities to care for those abandoned to die, providing care and comfort to people in their final days.

Regardless of how we might feel about this, health care for all has been and remains an inherently Christian notion. And it is a means through which God intervenes indirectly all the time in our lives to relieve pain and suffering and to restore health. It seems that God chooses to partner with people in bringing relief and restoring health, rather than repeatedly bypassing us to intervene dramatically and directly. Those who cure the sick today – and indeed all those who intervene to help in the form of humanitarian aid, counselling, vaccine development and rollout, disaster predication technologies and preventative measures to help 'build back better' next time – each extend the very hands of God.

Putting words to pain

I remember well the day when the parent of a child in my daughter's class ran to catch up with me in the school playground to tell me she had breast cancer. As I watched and walked with her through the battle with chemotherapy and radiotherapy over the following eighteen months, my friend showed me what it looks like to fight but also to patiently endure. The last time I saw her was during a visit to her home. We chatted and played music, and I asked if my friend would like me to read the Bible to her. After a moment of wracking my brains, I found myself opening the pages at Psalm 22:

> My God, my God, why have you forsaken me?
>> Why are you so far from saving me,
>> so far from my cries of anguish?
> My God, I cry out by day, but you do not answer,
>> by night, but I find no rest . . .
> I am poured out like water,
>> and all my bones are out of joint.
> My heart has turned to wax;
>> it has melted within me.
> My mouth is dried up like a potsherd,
>> and my tongue sticks to the roof of my mouth;
>> you lay me in the dust of death.[7]

As I began to read, I mentally kicked myself and asked why I hadn't thought to read Psalm 23 instead! Just one psalm further on, and you find much more comforting words:

> The LORD is my shepherd, I lack nothing.
>   He makes me lie down in green pastures,
> he leads me beside quiet waters,
>   he refreshes my soul . . .
> Even though I walk
>   through the darkest valley,
> I will fear no evil,
>   for you are with me;
> your rod and your staff,
>   they comfort me.[8]

Why hadn't I read those words instead? *Green pastures. Quiet waters. Refreshes my soul.* Who wouldn't want that? Yet, as I reflected later on that poignant final time together, it dawned on me that the words of Psalm 22 find resonance with a terminally ill cancer patient in a unique way. *Bones . . . out of joint. Mouth . . . dried up. Dust of death.* Once again, the pages of the Bible do not shy away from life's rawness. In fact, it is hard to find a form of suffering that we face today that is *not* mentioned there – depression, suicide, self-harm, physical illness, refugee crises, famine, plague, locusts, earthquakes, storms, wars and abuse of many kinds. It's all there, and it can be comforting to find words for our pain within words that others have used to talk to God about their anguish.

By his wounds we are healed

Psalm 22 also contains words that reach into the future as they describe the brutal crucifixion of Jesus Christ at the hands of Roman executioners. Jesus speaks the words of this psalm in his final hours on earth. When we run out of answers as to why God has or has not intervened in a situation in our lives, we are led to this place. To a wooden cross just outside Jerusalem in AD 33 on which Jesus the Messiah was nailed and died.

How does this help us? First, because it tells us that at the heart of the Christian faith is a God who *knows what it is to suffer.* He has not remained aloof or distant from the human plight, but has fully lowered and aligned himself with us, including by suffering like us. Crucifixion was a method of execution reserved for the lowest of the low, more degrading and brutal than any other method at any other point in history. The notion that God himself would end his days hanging from a cross was viewed with ridicule and mockery. Yet, if God has experienced this level of trauma, then something profound is available to us in our pain. The prophet Isaiah described Jesus as 'a man of suffering, and familiar with pain'.[9] When we bring our trauma and tragedy to him, we come to a God who *understands*, who *knows*, who *gets it*, because he himself has suffered *like us.*

Second, it tells us that God has intervened in our world in ways that go way beyond our expectations. An often-used aphorism states, 'The only thing necessary for the triumph of evil is for good men to do nothing.' In other words, without intervention, evil will triumph, and we see this happening all across the world in human systems and governments. But not so with God. That first Easter shows us that God hasn't done nothing in the face of evil; he has done everything needed to overcome evil. The apostle Paul, in a letter to the church in Colossae, describes what was happening at Calvary: 'having disarmed the powers and authorities, he made a public spectacle of them, triumphing over them by the cross'.[10] Humanly speaking, a public spectacle was being made of Jesus, but spiritually Jesus was making a public spectacle of the forces of evil. Disarming them. Dealing them a fatal blow. Taking the wind out of the sails of the evil one.

Jesus hasn't just suffered like us, but also *for us*. We are told that somehow his death benefits us, and that somehow 'by his wounds we are healed'.[11] This is often the point at which some fail to see how one man's death two thousand years ago benefits us today. But the worst suffering of Jesus was not the humiliation of being naked, or the flogging, or the agony of having nails driven through his hands and feet. The worst part was the cosmic isolation from the Father that came with carrying the weight of the world's evil on his innocent shoulders. This is a death unlike any other. A death upon which history hinges. A death that mends the broken relationship between people and God, and with the potential to mend our broken planet because it brings life to all who place their full trust in Jesus today. Somehow, when we were dead in our sins, the living Jesus took them upon himself. As Jesus died, we were made alive to God – forgiven and restored. That is, if we want to be. While we do not have the answers to why God does or does not intervene in specific situations, he has not left us on our own in our plight. He has intervened decisively in human history in the person of Jesus Christ to bring very real comfort and hope.

Can good come from a natural disaster?

We can also say that there are some good things that can come from times of suffering. Many of the stories shared in this book show how there can be beauty even amid tragic loss. Communities pull together, kindness is poured out, friendships go to new depths. Of course, we mustn't make the error of assuming that the good that can result from disaster is the *reason it happened*. There are catastrophes on this earth that are unfathomable here and now. To force reasons on a grieving person is only to add to that person's suffering. Nevertheless, there are sometimes good things that come out of suffering, over time, that have a refining effect on us and our communities. The apostle Paul, in his letter to the church in Rome, said that 'suffering produces perseverance; perseverance, character; and character, hope. And hope does not put us to shame, because God's love has been poured out into our hearts through the Holy Spirit, who has been given to us.'[12]

With moderate suffering, we grow more in courage, perseverance and patience when life is hard than when life is straightforward. Sometimes, God may allow trials because, through them, these good qualities can be expressed. We may also discover that our story encourages others who are walking through a similar valley. We may find ourselves 'comfort[ing] those in any trouble with the comfort we ourselves [have received]'.[13] In Rosie's story, her experience of the earthquake even precipitated a kind of spiritual awakening, leading her to a relationship with God.

Just like the man Job (see chapter 8), we are not always given *reasons* for our suffering, but we are offered a *relationship* – a friendship with God. Jesus was cut off from the Father in his hour of worst agony so that you and I need never be cut off from the love and comfort of God. Because Jesus died for us, whatever we face in life we need never face it alone. God has come close in Jesus, and for those who come close to him there is help available. There is strength we never knew we had and hope to face another day. Whatever you have believed up to this point, will you consider inviting this God to journey with you in your suffering?

One day he will intervene once and for all

On that first Good Friday, evil was defeated. Why then do we continue to see people's lives turned upside down by death and destruction? Because the forces of evil are still with us, but one day they will be removed once and for all.

One day, God will intervene once and for all in our world. This life is not all that there is. There is more to come. Summer is coming. In the modern world people hold varying views on the afterlife. Some believe that oblivion awaits, and people simply return to the earth. Others believe we enter a cycle of rebirth, but from which there is no guarantee of escape unless we work hard on ourselves. Still others may think that we float away to some cloud-based destination that holds little attraction. But the Bible speaks of heaven coming down to us, and of God dwelling with his people and making everything new. One day, Jesus will return, and the kingdom of God will be fully established on earth, bringing an end to strife, injustice, grief and sickness. Good wins. Evil loses. Justice will be meted out. People will answer to God for their lives, good or bad or both. The very end of the Bible paints a picture of this future, saying,

> They will be [God's] people, and God himself will be with them and be their God. 'He will wipe [away] every tear from their eyes. There will be no more death' or mourning or crying or pain, for the old order of things has passed away.[14]

The eye is one of the most delicate parts of the human body. As a mother I have often wiped away the tears of my children – something that takes tenderness, care and time. We are told that the Creator of the cosmos will do this for his people. What kind of God would do that? I wonder how long it will take? No tears from this life will go unnoticed because each person matters and is seen by God.

No more disasters and diseases?

There will be a new heaven and a new earth. Will this new earth be free from tsunami, earthquakes, storms and volcanic eruptions? Or will it be that we will no longer be harmed by natural disasters, especially since the inequalities that lead to poverty will be gone? Will it have mountain ranges and ocean trenches, ecosystems and desert islands? Will we be so in tune with nature's signs that we intuitively know when a cataclysm is coming and, rather than be taken by surprise, we position ourselves, and others, to watch it in all its glory? These are questions that remain unanswered. But whatever the truth is, the new heaven and new earth to come will be every bit as real as this one, and will be beautiful and good. Why? Because God will be at the centre.

Even our bodies will be transformed. We will not always have to contend with physical frailty and decline. Nor will we be confined to a ghostly existence somehow less real than the one we have now. Humans will have resurrected bodies that will be made new. Why do Christians believe this? Because Jesus did not remain dead. Easter Sunday followed Good Friday. The tomb became empty. Jesus started appearing to women and men telling them to tell others that he had risen from the grave, never to die again. You may not agree that Jesus really did rise from the dead, but there are many scholars and sceptics who have exhausted the alternatives and concluded that it must be true.[15] Their findings are worth a look.

Heavenly bodies

There was something familiar but also different about Jesus' resurrection body. There were the marks of nails in his hands and feet bearing witness to his death, but he could also move through walls and appear and disappear in front of his followers. There was both continuity and discontinuity with the body he'd had before. Jesus is said to be the forerunner, or the firstborn from among the dead. For all who believe in and follow him, the same will be true of us. The same Holy Spirit who raised Jesus to life also comes to live in the person who places his or her full trust in Christ. The apostle Paul, writing to the church in Corinth, put it like this, describing the bodies we have now as a bit like a seed that one day will grow into something new and better:

So will it be with the resurrection of the dead. The body that is sown is perishable, it is raised imperishable; it is sown in dishonour, it is raised in glory; it is sown in weakness, it is raised in power; it is sown a natural body, it is raised a spiritual body.

If there is a natural body, there is also a spiritual body.[16]

Bring your afflictions and addictions. Bring your scars and shame. Bring your weaknesses and limitations to the God who raises the dead. You will be transformed. There may be glimpses of this in this life for some. But for all who believe, resurrection will be a reality.

So why doesn't God intervene once and for all now? We see that he intervenes indirectly every day, through the work of all who help the sick and disaster-stricken. He has intervened in Jesus to defeat the powers of evil so that we can each know God with us in all that we face, and to show that one day there will be a world without suffering and death. One day, God will intervene to rid the world of every kind of evil and will restore our bodies and the natural world to their rightful order. We see signs of this future world every time someone is healed, and every time we see death and decay reversed in miraculous ways.

The reason why that final intervention hasn't taken place yet is to allow people time to decide what they believe. In a letter written by the apostle Peter, we read, 'The Lord is not slow in keeping his promise [to intervene], as some understand slowness. Instead he is patient with you, not wanting anyone to perish, but everyone to come to repentance.'[17]

No-one will be included in the new heaven and new earth who doesn't want to be there. God has given us the dignity of choice. What will you decide?

Earthquake, Japan 2016

Paul, pastor and founding CEO of Kyushu Christ Disaster Relief Centre

In 1995, Osaka and Kobe were struck by a massive earthquake. At that time, I was a senior student at a seminary in Tokyo, and leader of the student body. I had heard about the devastation and really wanted to go and help, but we were in the middle of term and it would have disrupted the teaching schedule, so I chose not to. In the vacation, I did eventually make it to Kobe, but by now two months had passed and it was clear that my offers of help were woefully late. Back in Tokyo, one of my pastors at seminary pointed out the problem: 'You were late because you have no prior experience. If you knew the suffering and havoc that earthquakes wreak, you would have gone straight away.' I was shocked by this, but it was true. This was my first negative and regrettable experience of disaster relief.

Sixteen years later, the biggest earthquake ever recorded in Japanese history (9.1 magnitude) struck the Tōhoku (northeast) region of Japan near Sendai, triggering a gigantic tsunami. Once again, I was praying and wondering if I should go or not. A phone call to my friend, chairman of Food for the Hungry at the time, was all it took to persuade me to do things differently this time. There was no petrol, so driving was out of the question. My friend collected me from the train and took me to the centre of the disaster area in Sendai to scenes that looked like the aftermath of an atomic bomb explosion. Total devastation. The 25-metre-high tsunami had flattened the city for miles.

I was stunned but had to keep moving and was quickly put to work in a school giving temporary shelter to those whose homes had been obliterated. For three days, I sorted and served food. It felt good to be helpful, but it also wasn't long before I made another mistake.

One evening, I noticed an elderly man on his own, so I went over to talk to him. Things initially went well, but after a while he noticed I had no name tag and became suspicious. I apologized for forgetting to bring my lanyard but assured him that I was genuine. The thing I didn't understand was that, immediately after the earthquake, people had evacuated their homes only to see them looted as criminals moved in to take advantage. Strangers were not trusted. The man I was trying to befriend became nervous and began to shout at me to leave. Even the leader of the shelter couldn't persuade him that I was a genuine volunteer, so I decided the best thing would be to put the man's wishes above my own. It was cold outside, but I took a blanket and slept in the car that night. Miserable and full of regrets, I asked myself what I was doing there. I had tried to help, but had ended up doing harm.

The next day I headed back to the centre looking for new ways to help. My friend, the chairman of Food for the Hungry, invited me to come along to a meeting with him. Church pastors met and prayed together with great excitement and energy as they planned how to bring help to Japanese disaster victims. At the time, I didn't realize the significance of what I was witnessing, but later understood that a new organization, Tōhoku Help, a disaster relief church network, had been founded. As time went on, this network became vast. That I was present the day it began would prove to be pivotal when I established my own organization five years later.

I returned to my home town of Fukuoka and to my role as a pastor but wanted to continue to bring help. After a natural disaster, this cannot simply be a one-off event. Continued help is needed, and the church is there to serve the community. But how exactly we should do this was not yet clear. In 2012, we began a project called Santa Project Kyushu, whose aim was to bring Christmas gifts to children in affected areas. Members of the community in Fukuoka brought gifts to the churches, and we carried them as presents, together with Santa Claus, to public elementary schools and kindergartens in Tōhoku. Santa Project Kyushu is still happening today.

Five years after Sendai came the Kumamoto earthquake of 2016. We felt this in my home town, Fukuoka, about 60 miles away. I called my friend in Kumamoto who had already started with the relief effort. Two days later, another big earthquake struck, affecting an even wider area. Both earthquakes were level 7, and it is unusual for two such massive quakes to occur consecutively. The epicentre, the Mashiki area, was devastated. I wanted to do something to help, even more so because the local churches that would want to help were themselves damaged and it was very important to stand with and help them.

I called every pastor I knew, and two days after the second quake people travelled from all over Japan to a national prayer gathering. There were about fifty of us. Out of this meeting, we founded a new organization, the Kyushu Christ Disaster Relief Centre, of which I was asked to be the CEO.

Other Christian disaster relief charities in Japan, such as World Vision, Food for the Hungry and Crash, came alongside and helped us. In the aftermath of the 2011 earthquake and tsunami in Tōhoku, they had tended to work separately, partly because the damage had affected such a vast area and there was no choice but to spread out. But this time, we were working together much more.

My friend, who was already leading the response of the local churches on the ground, became director of the disaster relief base. Initially, we focused on providing shelter, food, water and clothing – basic practical needs. Those whose houses had collapsed were given shelter in a local school gym before being moved to temporary housing two months later. In the early days, we simply went to the gym, asked people what they needed and provided it. We also had teams of nurses giving medical care to the injured.

Once the 'first response' was running smoothly, we started working with children. After two massive earthquakes the children were left traumatized and anxious. Moreover, their parents were struggling with their own stress and anxiety and were unable to console these little ones. We began with a teddy bear project. More than a hundred huggable soft toys were given out and had a profoundly comforting effect. We also started a club and invited local children along. At first, numbers were low, but we later heard that the American baseball player and Christian Dennis Sarfate would be playing at the stadium in Fukuoka, so we approached him about working together.

One month after the earthquakes, Dennis sent out an invitation for children to come to his game for free. He prepared special seats for the children and invited them onto the pitch to meet the team before the game. About fifty children accepted. For some it was a dream come true. Parents came along and were greatly moved watching their kids smiling and laughing. The newspapers and TV stations picked up the story. All in all, it was a hugely memorable evening, and we began to be trusted by the local community.

The Kumamoto earthquake of 2016 killed at least fifty people, injured three thousand and caused at least forty-four thousand to flee their homes. Unsafe houses needed to be cleared out before they were demolished and rebuilt, and we were involved in this. Some buildings were on the verge of collapse and too dangerous to enter, but others were less risky, so we worked within the Government guidelines. But Japanese people have a culture of shame and were mortified at the prospect of a stranger seeing their house in a messy state. Even though they were in a terrible situation and needed help, and even though we had distributed handouts to say we were there to help, they still didn't want us to enter their homes. It was very hard to establish trust. But at one house in particular, the owners were brave enough to reach out. As we went in, the neighbours surrounded the house. They were watching us and we them. The delight and appreciation of the owners had a ripple effect and, one by one, we had the opportunity to serve in other homes.

Our volunteers became known in the town as Mr Christ or Mrs Christ, related to the fact that our name is Kyushu Christ Disaster Relief Centre. As the organization grew, volunteers began to join us from other countries as well as from across

Japan. It was hard to remember individual names, so they just called us Mr Christ and Mrs Christ. Some people would come for just one day, and others for much longer. The locals could see that, even though the volunteers were different, they were all working towards the same goal. Each one was there to help, each one was part of the global family of God, and identified by the name of Christ.

10

What should my response be to a natural disaster?

Thanks to the Internet and social media, it never takes more than a few minutes to hear about the next emergency. We rarely go for more than a few weeks without news of another catastrophe, be it a natural or a national disaster. The global village in which we now live can leave us feeling overwhelmed and suffering from compassion fatigue, and it is hard to know how to respond. What should our response be to a disaster? Paul's story may resonate. Many of us would like to help in some way but don't really know how. There are, however, some very practical things that we can do to help to be part of the solution to relieving suffering caused by natural and national disasters.

Environmental care

The interdependence of humans and nature was highlighted during the lockdown of 2020, a time when the noise generated by the human race was hushed to an unprecedented low. This provided a unique opportunity for ecologists and conservationists to take note of how creatures responded when noise pollution was at a minimum. Scientists writing in the journal *Science* noticed that certain types of bird changed their songs completely.[1] In the San Francisco Bay area, the white-crowned sparrow began to sing a much deeper, richer song. Prior to lockdown, the sparrow had resorted to a simple tune that could be belted out at top volume and heard above traffic, chatter, roadworks and so on. But with urban noise gone, the white-crowned sparrow could afford a more embellished, Pavarotti-style melody. Volume was replaced by quality.

This then made me wonder: how else is human activity somehow 'muting' or changing the natural world? Of course, we have become aware of multiple different ways in which this happens. Copious quantities of plastic are being swallowed by marine creatures. Melting icebergs leave penguins and polar bears stranded or else exhausted from swimming. Poaching and aggressive fishing have pushed many kinds of sea life and wildlife to the brink of extinction. Needless deforestation has destroyed habitats and whole ecosystems, as well as precipitating landslides and desertification. All in the space of a few decades. We are plundering our planet like no other generation and at a rate that experts tell us will slide us into something that is catastrophic and irreversible. Is that what we want for ourselves, and for our children and grandchildren? It isn't too late to turn things around, but we have a matter of years to do it. We each have a part to play.

There are different motivations for caring for the natural world. Some might see the need to care for our habitat as a humanist initiative, because nature is all that we have, and people are uniquely placed to make a difference. Others might take the view that nature has divine status or a consciousness of its own akin to that of 'mother nature'. It may surprise some to know that care for the environment is a virtue that is also central to Christian belief. Even organizations such as that which became the RSPCA have their origins in Christian belief.[2] Granted, some strands of Christianity hold that, since believers have a ticket to heaven, the state of the earth is of little importance. When Jesus returns, we can start again. Yet the opening chapters of Genesis give a very different message. *Homo sapiens* are given a unique status in the created order. They are said to be made in the 'image' of God, and are instructed by God to look after the natural world:

God blessed [humankind] and said to them, 'Be fruitful and increase in number; fill the earth and subdue it. Rule over the fish in the sea and the birds in the sky and over every living creature that moves on the ground.'[3]

Some express concern that these instructions to 'rule over' may provide grounds for egotism and exploitation of natural resources for self-serving ends. Quite the opposite. Humans are asked to exercise stewardship – one of dominion not domination. The notion of 'bearing the image' of another has undertones of a sense of responsibility. In the Ancient Near East, the context in which Genesis 1 was written, images of the king were placed in towns and cities as a reminder of the king's authority and that citizens were accountable to him. Similarly, to be bearers of God's image serves to remind people that God is sovereign and we are his representatives or ambassadors. Our privileged position comes with a responsibility to care for and be stewards of our natural habitat, mindful that we must ultimately answer to God for this when he returns to make all things new. The urgency of the environmentalist cry for people to play their part in cleaning up the mess we have made of things and to provide a sustainable habitat for the generations to come entirely aligns with Christian belief.

This responsibility extends into many other areas as well, encompassing animal welfare, ecology, sustainable farming and fishing, the ending of illegal poaching, and care for endangered species. If all humans are made in the image of God, then we do not have a licence to simply please ourselves; we carry a responsibility to use our position for the flourishing of all other living things.

There are all kinds of practical outworkings here. To what extent am I living in a way that shows care for my natural habitat and for the next generation who will inherit it? How big is my carbon footprint, and my use of plastics? What changes could I make to better steward natural resources?

Altruism

It was Jesus who said, 'So in everything, do to others what you would have them do to you, for this sums up the Law and the Prophets.'[4]

Whatever we might make of his divinity, there is a wisdom and a timelessness to these words that have undergirded human rights laws around the world. If each person is precious to God, then every life matters, and a helpful gauge as we think about our response to disasters is to ask ourselves how we would like to be treated if the tables were turned. This is a principle for every area of daily life. Living for the good of others, altruism, stems from the ethics of Jesus and was embodied in his very life and death.

In chapter 1 we mentioned philosopher Peter Singer, who is a vocal advocate of altruism and of helping people to contribute in the most effective way they can to make the biggest difference to the lives of others. He describes the aim of his charity, Effective Altruism, as follows:

Most of us want to make a difference. We see suffering, injustice and death, and are moved to do something about them. But working out what that 'something' is, let alone actually doing it, can be a difficult and disheartening challenge. Effective altruism is a response to this challenge. It is a research field which uses high-quality evidence and careful reasoning to work out how to help others as much as possible. It is also a community of people taking these answers seriously by focusing their efforts on the most promising solutions to the world's most pressing problems.[5]

Singer highlights some important points. Some may make the biggest difference through financial giving, whereas others may need to establish new organizations or join existing ones. Some may need to receive training and join a team of first responders. Others may have a role in supporting those returning with trauma as a result of the things they have seen. Still others have a part to play through the use of their skills and expertise in developing technologies. After all, we are greatly indebted to the scientists who produced a COVID-19 vaccine within eighteen months instead of the usual ten years. Or we could call to mind Alan Turing, whose breaking of the Enigma code helped to shorten the Second World War. His biggest contribution by far was to stay at home and use his existing skills to relieve the suffering of others.

Some may want to raise awareness by lobbying or petit-ioning governments, be it about the housing of refugees, carbon emissions or the international aid budget. Others will be moved to petition or boycott certain high street clothing companies whose working conditions in sweatshops are substandard, even dangerous, and keep others in poverty and possibly even in forms of slavery. They succeed in doing so because we in the West continue to buy their products. Change comes when whole swathes of people get on board. Some of us need to examine our shopping habits and ask, what does it mean to be an altruistic high street consumer? We may need to read up on the ethical practices of different shops and clothing brands. The lowest price for us is rarely good news for the person who made it.

Whatever our contribution may be, there are things that all of us can do. One thing that everyone can do is to give financially to charities and organizations working in disaster areas. Singer encourages those who have the means to give 10% of their income to worthy causes. Tithing of time, resources and money, in proportion to income, has been a practice in Jewish and Christian communities for centuries, and those who trust God with their finances are told they will have all that they need.

Which charity?

Of course, the difficulty can be in knowing which charity to give to. The encouragement from those working in this area is not simply to give blindly, but to take time to research dif-ferent charities. There are some smaller agencies that provide high-quality work in disaster zones, whereas larger agencies can sometimes be slower and less efficient due to political and bureaucratic challenges. In the course of researching an agency we are encouraged to do the following:

- Check their records, including their financial history, ethical history, policies, alliances, and their quality standards certifications, such as ISO 9001 or Core Humanitarian Standard (CHS).
- Ask questions about where they are serving and why. Are they meeting the most critical needs in the worst-affected areas?
- Take time to call the agency directly. Speaking with current or former staff can help you match your personal passions and calling with the agency you support.

We each have a part to play in helping those who suffer as a result of natural and national disasters. The challenge is to take time to work out how we can each make the biggest difference.

Spiritual questions

During the first wave of the COVID-19 pandemic, the UK was locked down over spring and early summer. People were allowed to leave their houses only for essential shopping and one session of exercise. I remember running in the park mindful of the new etiquette of keeping a safe distance and certainly not coughing while in the vicinity of another human being. Verbal greetings *became impolite* because of the risk of viral transmission.

On one occasion, as a couple ran past a man who was out walking, they got a little bit too close and began to be yelled at by him: 'Why can't you just go home and stop making trouble for us all!' The response from one of the runners was, 'Why don't you stop complaining and let us get on with it!' The man shouted back, 'I don't want to die, OK?'

The fear in this man was tangible and representative of how many were feeling. COVID-19 has reminded us of some important truths about our humanity. First, that life is precious yet fragile – it can end in a matter of days. Second, that relationships are vital to our well-being, and long periods of isolation are not good for us. The natural disaster that we have all just been through, and indeed the ones we see on our screens, can cause all kinds of questions to arise in us. *What is life really all about? If my life were to end suddenly, am I at peace with how I've lived and with where I'm headed? Is there a way to live free from the fear of 'What if . . . ?'*

A BBC article noted that there has been a resurgence of interest in matters of faith and spirituality as a result of the pandemic,[6] even though in the preceding years religious life was in decline. It is important not to squash our questions but to take time to ask them and weigh the responses we receive from different viewpoints. The Christian faith has some important things to say on these matters, and courses such as *Alpha*[7] and *Christianity Explored*[8] provide a helpful way to journey with others who are asking similar questions of life and faith. As someone who became a Christian aged twenty, I found this a vital process. Perhaps part of your response to natural disasters might be to allow your questions to bubble to the surface, and to find a way to discuss them with like-minded people. You may have friends who are Christians or be aware of a local church, and these are good places to begin the journey. There are also books and websites which may be helpful.[9]

If it's true that Jesus rose from the dead, then this life is not all that there is. There is more than we can see with our eyes. Life is precious and it will continue on if we take the hand of Jesus. If it's true that Jesus has defeated our worst enemy, then it's also true that whoever follows him will live on and will ultimately be resurrected and restored to a new heaven and new earth. Jesus said, 'I am the resurrection and the life. The one who believes in me will live, even though they die; and whoever lives by believing in me will never die. Do you believe this?'[10]

There is life beyond even the worst catastrophe at home or abroad, and so it's possible to live free from the dread of our worst fears coming true. Even more than that, we are promised *life before death*. In the here and now, dead things can be brought to life with Jesus involved. If we invite him into our life, there is hope for every person in every situation. Jesus has come to us so that we might have abundant life.

We are relational beings not just because we need other people but because we are hard-wired to relate to our Maker and will never truly be at rest until this relationship is restored. The story has been told of how two Italians who had been neighbours for most of their lives finally noticed each other during one of the lockdowns and went on to get engaged.[11] It took a global pandemic to connect two people who lived just metres apart. What will it take to restore you to a friendship with the God who loves you and is already with you?

However broken your experience of this planet may be, there is a God who longs to forgive you, comfort you and walk with you every day of your life. If you turn to him, you will discover new life and wholeness that go far beyond anything that this world can offer.

Tsunami, Sri Lanka 2004: evening

Rosi, tourist

By early evening on 26 December, we were told we'd be airlifted to Colombo. We had to make our way back down to the beach, and it was disconcerting to be so close to the sea again, watching the debris float by and waiting. As we swung up into the sky, I had to hold onto my son for dear life. Anytime I see a helicopter now, it immediately reminds me of this rescue, of being just plucked out and taken to safety. After a few days in Colombo to get passports and buy clothes, we flew back to the UK. All the big airlines were flying people out, whether they had a ticket or not.

Surviving a disaster like that left me incredibly grateful for every minute of life. I was just so thankful for every breath, and compared with simply being alive, everything else seemed so insignificant. The gift of life was everything. I was on a kind of high and wanted it to stay like that. But at the same time, I was also traumatized. We didn't end up having any formal counselling. I stayed in contact with some of the people we met on the day of the tsunami, and there was some comfort in remembering our shared experiences. It seemed to validate the event in a way, because I found myself wondering if the tsunami had really happened, or was it all just a bad dream? I think I did have some mild post-traumatic stress disorder rumbling away and didn't really sort it out in a formal way. For me, time and prayer has been the great healer.

Several months after we'd returned to Sudan, our home at the time, my British Council Library card was sent back to me via the British Council in Khartoum, returned to me by a Sri Lankan fisherman. This man had lost his fishing boat and I was humbled that he had gone to such lengths to find me halfway across the world, to return a library card. My instinct was to try to find a way to thank him. We were able to contribute towards a fund to help restore the village and the hotel where we'd stayed in Dikwella. A couple of years later, my parents visited and reported back that the owners had rebuilt and were back in business.

I shared my story on the website of MedAir, our employer at the time, and several people wrote in, asking who I thought I was to be sharing a story of rescue when hundreds of thousands of people had lost their lives? This was really difficult for me. I totally understood this perspective. There are so many questions. Why? Why did we survive? Why did God let that happen? What happened to all those other people? I'm no better than any of the people who lost their lives, but somehow God helped and rescued us that day. Sometimes I feel that I should be doing something incredible to justify the fact that we made it out alive, but when I'm calm and thinking things through with the God I know, I don't think he is asking that of me. All I can cling to is the reality that he had personally communicated his presence to me that day. We don't have the answers, and it's not up to me or anything I've done, but God has shown me again and again that he is good, and can be trusted.

Survivor's guilt is real and it's tempting to stay silent. But I can only tell my story, our story, as it is.

Notes

Introduction

1 '2005 Hurricane Katrina: Facts, FAQs, and How to Help', World Vision, last updated 25 November 2019, <https://www. worldvision.org/disaster-relief-news-stories/2005-hurricane-katrina-facts>.

2 Allison Plyer, 'Facts for Features: Katrina Impact', The Data Center, 26 August 2016, <https://www.datacenterresearch.org/ data-resources/katrina/facts-for-impact/>.

1 If God is real, why are there natural disasters?

1 Ian Woolverton, 'We Have Too Many Bodies', *The Guardian*, 12 January 2005, <https://www.theguardian.com/society/2005/ jan/12/internationalaidanddevelopment.indianoceantsunamide cember2004>.

2 Martin Kettle, 'How Can Religious People Explain Something Like This?', *The Guardian*, 28 December 2004, <https://www. theguardian.com/environment/2004/dec/28/religion.comment>.

3 Ron Rosenbaum, 'Disaster Ignites Debate: "Was God in the Tsunami?"', 10 January 2005, *The Observer*, <https://observer.com/ 2005/01/disaster-ignites-debate-was-god-in-the-tsunami/>.

4 'Stephen Fry on God: The Meaning of Life', RTÉ One, 28 January 2015, YouTube, <https://www.youtube.com/ watch?v=-suvkwNYSQo>.

5 David Hume, *Dialogues Concerning Natural Religion* (1779; London: Penguin, [n.d.]), p. 186.

6 Alvin Plantinga, *God, Freedom and Evil* (Grand Rapids, MI: Eerdmans, 1974).

7 National Geographic, 'Earthquakes 101', 6 December 2015, YouTube, <https://www.youtube.com/watch?v=e7ho6z32yyo>.

8 Kettle, 'How Can Religious People Explain Something Like This?'

9 Naina Bajekal, 'Want to Do More Good? This Movement Might Have the Answer', *Time*, 10 August 2022, <https://time.com/6204627/effective-altruism-longtermism-william-macaskill-interview/>.

10 'Peter Singer: How Can We Be More Effective Altruists?', *TED Radio Hour*, NPR, 26 May 2017, <https://www.npr.org/2017/05/26/529958027/peter-singer-how-can-we-be-more-effective-altruists?t=1659959916781>.

11 Plato, *Gorgias*, Part 2, in *The Dialogues of Plato: Gorgias; Philebus; Parmenides; Theaetetus; Sophist; Statesman* (New York: Scribner, Armstrong, 1878), p. 72.

12 Aristotle, *Politics*, tr. H. Rackham, Loeb Classical Library 264, pp. 20–21, <https://www.loebclassics.com/view/LCL264/1932/volume.xml>.

13 Tom Holland, *Dominion* (London: Abacus, 2020).

14 E. J. Wielenberg, 'In Defense of Non-Natural, Non-Theistic Moral Realism', *Faith and Philosophy*, 26/1 (2009), p. 26.

15 J. P. Moreland and William Lane Craig, *Philosophical Foundations for a Christian Worldview* (Downers Grove, IL: InterVarsity Press, 2003), p. 492.

16 W. J. Wainwright, 'In Defense of Non-Natural Theistic Realism: A Response to Wielenberg', *Faith and Philosophy*, 27/4 (2010), pp. 457–463.

2 Is this the best of all possible worlds?

1 Gottfried W. Leibniz, *Theodicy: Essays on the Goodness of God, the Freedom of Man and the Origin of Evil*, ed. A. M. Farrer,

tr. E. M. Huggard (Chicago & La Salle, IL: Open Court, 1985). (French orig., *Théodicée* [1710].)

2 Voltaire, 'Poem on the Lisbon Disaster; or An Inquiry into the Axiom "All Is Well"', 1756; tr. Antony Lyon, 2013, revised 2013, <https://static1.squarespace.com/static/55316a91e4b06d7c3b435f17/t/5f0b98212d6235002623d7dd/1594595362627/Voltaire+-+Poem+on+the+Lisbon+Disaster.pdf>. Reproduced by kind permission.

3 P. van Inwagen, 'Modal Epistemology', *Philosophical Studies*, 92 (1988), pp. 67–84.

4 R. S. Saunders et al., 'Magellan Mission Summary', *Journal of Geophysical Research Planets* 97/E8 (1992), pp. 13067–13090; J. E. Guest et al., 'Small Volcanic Edifices and Volcanism in the Plains of Venus', *Journal of Geophysical Research* 97/E10 (1992), pp. 15949–15966.

5 'The Planet Venus', NASA Education, last updated 9 April 2009, <https://www.nasa.gov/audience/forstudents/5-8/features/F_The_Planet_Venus_5-8.html>.

6 Hannah Devlin, 'Scientists Identify Rain of Molten Iron on Distant Exoplanet', *The Guardian*, 11 March 2020, <https://www.theguardian.com/science/2020/mar/11/scientists-identify-rain-of-molten-iron-on-distant-exoplanet/>.

7 Immanuel Kant, 'On the Causes of Earthquakes on the Occasion of the Calamity that Befell the Western Countries of Europe towards the End of Last Year,' Essay, 1 January 1756.

8 Alfred Wegener, *Die Entstehung der Kontinente und Ozeane* [The origin of continents and oceans] (Brunswick: Vieweg & Sohn, 1915).

9 Shannon Hall, 'Earth's Tectonic Activity May Be Crucial for Life – and Rare in Our Galaxy', *Scientific American*, 20 July 2017, <https://www.scientificamerican.com/article/earths-tectonic-activity-may-be-crucial-for-life-and-rare-in-our-galaxy/>.

10 Peter Ward and Donald Brownlee, *Rare Earth* (New York: Copernicus, 2004).

11 Robert S. White, *Who Is to Blame? Disasters, Nature and Acts of God* (Oxford: Monarch, 2014), p. 27.

12 Ibid., p. 28.

13 P. van Inwagen, 'The Magnitude, Duration and Distribution of Evil', in *God, Knowledge, and Mystery* (Ithaca, NY: Cornell University Press, 1995), p. 118; R. Swinburne, *Providence and the Problem of Evil* (Oxford: OUP, 1998); J. Polkinghorne, *Exploring Reality: The Intertwining of Science and Religion* (London: SPCK, 2005), p. 143.

14 Van Inwagen, 'Modal Epistemology', pp. 67–84.

15 Stephen J. Wykstra, 'The Human Obstacle to Evidential Arguments from Suffering: On Avoiding the Evils of "Appearance"', *International Journal for Philosophy of Religion*, 16 (1984), pp. 73–93.

3 Why do *so many* suffer and die in natural disasters?

1 Michael Le Page, 'Hurricane Dorian Is Joint Strongest Atlantic Storm Ever to Hit Land', *New Scientist*, 2 September 2019, <https://www.newscientist.com/article/2214937-hurricane-dorian-is-joint-strongest-atlantic-storm-ever-to-hit-land/>.

2 Soutik Biswas, 'Amphan: Why Bay of Bengal Is the World's Hotbed of Tropical Cyclones', BBC News online, 19 May 2020, <https://www.bbc.co.uk/news/world-asia-india-52718531>.

3 William Rowe, 'The Problem of Evil and Some Varieties of Atheism', *American Philosophical Quarterly*, 16 (1979), pp. 335–341.

4 Paul Draper, 'Pain and Pleasure: An Evidential Problem for Theists', *Noûs*, 23 (1989), pp. 331–350.

5 Roger Abbott, '"I Will Show You My Faith by My Works": Addressing the Nexus between Philosophical Theodicy and Human Suffering and Loss in Contexts of "Natural" Disaster', *Religions*, 10/3 (2019), n. p.

6 Jean-Jacques Rousseau, *Emile, Or Treatise on Education*, Book 1 (1762), cited at '*Emile, or On Education*', Wikipedia, <https://en.wikipedia.org/wiki/Emile,_or_On_Education>.

7 Samir Ben Yahmed, 'Population Growth and Disasters', *World Health*, May–June 1994, p. 26, <https://apps.who.int/iris/bitstream/handle/10665/328006/WH-1994-May-Jun-p26-27-eng.pdf>.

8 Robert S. White, *Who Is to Blame? Disasters, Nature and Acts of God* (Oxford: Monarch, 2014), p. 16.

9 S. Amrith, *Crossing the Bay of Bengal: The Furies of Nature and the Fortunes of Migrants* (Cambridge, MA: Harvard University Press, 2013).

10 Sameh Wahba and Swarna Kazi, 'Bangladesh: Building Resilience in the Eye of the Storm (Part 3/3)', ReliefWeb (OCHA), 1 August 2017, <https://reliefweb.int/report/bangladesh/bangladesh-building-resilience-eye-storm-part-33>.

11 U. Haque et al., 'Reduced Death Rates from Cyclones in Bangladesh: What More Needs to Be Done?', *Bulletin of the World Health Organization*, 90/2 (1 Feb. 2012), pp. 150–156.

12 C. B. Field et al. (eds.), *Managing the Risks of Extreme Events and Disasters to Advance Climate Change Adaptation: A Special Report of Working Groups I and II of the Intergovernmental Panel on Climate Change* (Cambridge: Cambridge University Press, 2012).

13 Government figures appear to be higher than those from external sources. A death toll of between 100,000 and 250,000 is estimated.

14 White, *Who Is to Blame?* p. 72.

15 Kate Ravilious, 'Why the Haiti Quake Killed So Many', *New Scientist*, 19 January 2010, <https://www.newscientist.com/ article/dn18406-why-the-haiti-quake-killed-so-many/>.

16 Christina Nunez and National Geographic Staff, 'Sea Level Rise, Explained', *National Geographic*, 15 February 2022, <https://www.nationalgeographic.com/environment/article/ sea-level-rise-1>.

17 Tom Knutson, 'Global Warming and Hurricanes', GFDL, 12 July 2022, <https://www.gfdl.noaa.gov/global-warming-and- hurricanes/>.

18 Nunez and National Geographic Staff, 'Sea Level Rise, Explained'.

19 Somini Sengupta, 'Intense Arctic Wildfires Set a Pollution Record', *New York Times*, last updated 14 September 2020, <https://www.nytimes.com/2020/07/07/climate/climate- change-arctic-fires.html>.

20 'Climate Change: More Than 3bn Could Live in Extreme Heat by 2070', BBC News online, 5 May 2020, <https://www.bbc.co.uk/ news/science-environment-52543589>.

21 Knutson, 'Global Warming and Hurricanes'; Sarah Gibbens, 'How Warm Oceans Supercharge Deadly Hurricanes', *National Geographic*, 6 September 2019, <https://www.nationalgeographic. co.uk/environment-and-conservation/2019/09/how-warm- oceans-supercharge-deadly-hurricanes>.

22 T. M. Lenton et al., 'Climate Tipping Points – Too Risky to Bet Against', *Nature*, 27 November 2019, <https://www.nature.com/ articles/d41586-019-03595-0>.

23 'IPCC Report: "Code Red" for Human Driven Global Heating, Warns UN Chief', UN News, 9 August 2021, <https:// news.un.org/en/story/2021/08/1097362>.

24 Norman Miller, 'The Animals That Detect Disasters', quoting Irina Rafliana of the UNISDR, BBC Future Planet, 15 February 2022, <https://www.bbc.com/future/article/20220211-the-animals-that-predict-disasters>.

Wildfires, Australia 2019–20

1 Rebecca Abbott, 'Prayer Saved Thousands in Mallacoota, Claims "Atheist"', Eternity News, 7 January 2020, <https://www.eternitynews.com.au/australia/prayer-saved-thousands-in-mallacoota-claims-atheist/>.

4 Are natural disasters the judgment of God?

1 Cited in A. J. Conyers, *The Eclipse of Heaven* (Downers Grove, IL: InterVarsity Press, 1992), p. 13.

2 David Pawson, *Why Does God Allow Natural Disasters?* (n.p.: Anchor Recordings, 2014), p. 95.

3 Ibid., p .95.

4 Australian Associated Press, 'Israel Folau under Fire for Implying Bushfires Are God's Punishment', *The Guardian*, 18 November 2019, <https://www.theguardian.com/sport/2019/nov/18/israel-folau-says-bushfires-and-drought-are-gods-punishment-for-same-sex-marriage-and-abortion>.

5 Ian Woolverton, 'We Have Too Many Bodies', *The Guardian*, 12 January 2005, <https://www.theguardian.com/society/2005/jan/12/internationalaidanddevelopment.indianoceantsunamidecember2004>.

6 William Rowe, 'The Problem of Evil and Some Varieties of Atheism', *American Philosophical Quarterly*, 16 (1979), pp. 335–341; Paul Draper, 'Pain and Pleasure: An Evidential Problem for Theists', *Noûs*, 23 (1989), pp. 331–350.

7 Martin Kettle, 'How Can Religious People Explain Something Like This?', *The Guardian*, 28 December 2004, <https://www.theguardian.com/environment/2004/dec/28/religion.comment>.

8 Voltaire, 'Poem on the Lisbon Disaster; or An Inquiry into the Axiom "All Is Well"', 1756; tr. Antony Lyon, 2013, revised 2013, <https://static1.squarespace.com/static/55316a91e4b06d7c3b435f17/t/5f0b98212d6235002623d7dd/1594595362627/Voltaire+-+Poem+on+the+Lisbon+Disaster.pdf>.

9 Gen. 6:5–7.

10 Gen. 19:24–25.

11 Exod. 7 – 11.

12 Amos 1 – 9.

13 Erwin W. Lutzer, *An Act of God? Answers to Tough Questions about God's Role in Natural Disasters* (Carol Stream, IL: Tyndale House, 2011), pp. 45–46.

14 Acts 27:14.

15 Gen. 12; 26; Ruth 1; 2 Sam. 21; Acts 11.

16 Gen. 41 – 50.

17 Luke 13:1–5.

18 Luke 21:10–11, 25.

19 From Lutzer, *An Act of God?* p. 114.

20 Luke 13:6–9.

5 Can science now answer all of our questions?

1 Jessica Ball, 'Mount Vesuvius – Italy', Geology.com, <https://geology.com/volcanoes/vesuvius/>.

2 Jack Williams, 'The Epic Volcano Eruption That Led to the "Year without a Summer"', *Washington Post*, 10 June 2016, <https://www.washingtonpost.com/news/capital-weather-gang/wp/2015/04/24/the-epic-volcano-eruption-that-led-to-the-year-without-a-summer/>.

3 Bill Bryson, *A Brief History of Nearly Everything* (New York: Random House, 2003), p. 221.

4 'Hurricanes Are Named after HURACÁN the Mayan God of Wind, Fire and Storms', *Yucatan Times*, 17 August 2019, <https://www.theyucatantimes.com/2019/08/hurricanes-are-named-after-huracan-the-mayan-god-of-wind-fire-and-storms/>.

5 Encyclopaedia Britannica, 'Vulcan: Roman God', last updated 25 August 2021, <https://www.britannica.com/topic/Vulcan>.

6 'Typhoon (n.)', Online Etymology Dictionary, last updated 5 July 2018, <https://www.etymonline.com/word/typhoon>.

7 Robert Graves, *The Greek Myths* (New York: Penguin, 1955), ch. 36.

8 Gen. 1:1.

9 David Wilkinson, *The Message of Creation*, The Bible Speaks Today Series (Nottingham: Inter-Varsity Press, 2002), p. 18.

10 Gen. 1:16.

11 C. S. Lewis, *Miracles* (New York: Simon & Schuster, 1996), p. 140. *Miracles* by C. S. Lewis © copyright 1947, 1960 C. S. Lewis Pte Ltd. Extract used with permission.

12 For a more detailed discussion of science and God I recommend John Lennox, *Can Science Explain Everything?* (Epsom: Good Book Company, 2019).

13 Lamiat Sabin, 'Iceland: Volcano Near Reykjavik Erupts for Second Time in 6,000 Years', *The Independent*, 3 August 2022, <https://www.independent.co.uk/news/world/europe/fagradalsfjall-volcano-erupts-iceland-reykjavik-b2137536.html>.

14 Ps. 19:1.

6 Natural disasters or national disasters?

1 Yuval Noah Harari, *Homo Deus: A Brief History of Tomorrow* (London: Harvill Secker, 2016), p. 2.

2 Ibid., p. 3.

3 Rom. 8:20–22.

4 Rev. 21:5.

5 Rom. 8:20.

6 Gen. 3:1.

7 Richard Swinburne, *The Existence of God* (2nd edn; Oxford: OUP, 2004), chapter 11.

8 Gen. 3:16a.

9 Gen. 3:17.

10 S. Webb, *The Dome of Eden* (Eugene, OR: Wipf & Stock, 2010).

11 W. A. Dembski, *The End of Christianity: Finding a Good God in an Evil World* (Nashville, TN: Broadman & Holman, 2009).

12 Michael Lloyd, 'The Cosmic Fall and the Free Will Defence' (D.Phil. thesis, University of Oxford, 1997).

13 Gregory A. Boyd, *Satan and the Problem of Evil: Constructing a Trinitarian Warfare Theodicy* (Downers Grove, IL: InterVarsity Press, 2001).

14 E.g. C. S. Lewis, *The Problem of Pain* (London: Centenary Press, 1940); Alvin Plantinga, 'Supralapsarianism, or "O Felix Culpa"', in Peter van Inwagen (ed.), *Christian Faith and the Problem of Evil* (Grand Rapids, MI: Eerdmans, 2004), pp. 1–25.

15 David Bentley Hart, *The Doors of the Sea: Where Was God in the Tsunami?* (Chicago: Eerdmans, 2011), pp. 61–62.

16 Aleksandr Solzhenitsyn, *The Gulag Archipelago, 1918–56* (1st edn; London: Harvill Press, 2003), Part 4, 'The Ascent and Our Muzzled Freedom'.

17 Christopher Southgate, *The Groaning of Creation* (Louisville, KY: Westminster John Knox Press, 2008); Denis Alexander, *Creation or Evolution: Do We Have to Choose?* (Oxford: Monarch, 2008); John Polkinghorne, *Exploring Reality: The Intertwining of Science and Religion* (London: SPCK, 2005). See also John Cottingham's 'Dust of the earth' view expressed

in *The Spiritual Dimension* (Cambridge: CUP, 2005); Bethany Sollereder, *God, Evolution, and Animal Suffering: Theodicy without a Fall* (Abingdon: Routledge, 2019).

18 Dembski, *End of Christianity*; Webb, *Dome of Eden*.

19 M. J. Murray, *Nature Red in Tooth and Claw* (Oxford: OUP, 2008).

20 John 12:24.

21 Rom. 5:12.

22 Southgate, *Groaning of Creation*; Alexander, *Creation or Evolution*.

23 C. Southgate, 'Cosmic Evolution and Evil', in C. Meister and P. Moser (eds.), *The Cambridge Companion to the Problem of Evil*, Cambridge Companions to Religion (Cambridge: Cambridge University Press, 2017), pp. 147–164.

24 Gen. 2:16–17.

25 Gen. 3:16.

26 Alexander, *Creation or Evolution*.

27 Isa. 11:6–9.

28 Rom. 8:19.

29 Ps. 34:18.

30 John 6:35.

31 Matt. 27:51–52.

32 Matt. 28:1–2.

7 What about insects that devastate?

1 Samuel Okiror, 'Second Wave of Locusts in East Africa Said to Be 20 Times Worse', *The Guardian*, 13 April 2020, <https://www.theguardian.com/global-development/2020/apr/13/second-wave-of-locusts-in-east-africa-said-to-be-20-times-worse>.

2 Haley Cohen Gilliland, 'Gigantic New Locust Swarms Hit East Africa', *National Geographic*, 14 May 2020, <https://www.

nationalgeographic.co.uk/environment-and-conservation/
2020/05/gigantic-new-locust-swarms-hit-east-africa>.

3 Keith Cressman, 'Desert Locust Information Service', UN Food
and Agriculture Organization, <https://www.fao.org/ag/locusts/
common/ecg/190/en/1209_IRI_FAOCaseStudyDLIS.pdf>.

4 BBC News online, 'Hundreds of Billions of Locusts Swarm
in East Africa', 10 March 2020, <https://www.bbc.co.uk/news/
in-pictures-51618188>.

5 'Stephen Fry on God: The Meaning of Life', RTÉ One,
28 January 2015, YouTube, <https://www.youtube.com/
watch?v=-suvkwNYSQo>.

6 Riazat Butt, 'Attenborough Reveals Creationist Hate Mail for
Not Crediting God', *The Guardian*, 27 January 2009, <https://
www.theguardian.com/world/2009/jan/27/david-attenborough-
science>; John Plunkett, 'Attenborough: BBC Nature Shows
at Risk', *The Guardian*, 21 January 2008, <https://www.
theguardian.com/media/2008/jan/21/bbc.television2>.

7 'Parasites: Loiasis', Centers for Disease Control and Prevention,
<https://www.cdc.gov/parasites/loiasis/index.html>.

8 World Health Organization, 'Onchocerciasis', 11 January
2022, <https://www.who.int/news-room/fact-sheets/detail/
onchocerciasis>.

9 World Health Organization, 'The Top 10 Causes of Death',
9 December 2020, <https://www.who.int/news-room/fact-sheets/
detail/the-top-10-causes-of-death>.

10 Melinda Gates, *The Moment of Lift: How Empowering Women
Changes the World* (London: Bluebird, 2019), pp. 14–15.

11 Emily Osterloff, 'What Do Wasps Do?', Natural History
Museum, <https://www.nhm.ac.uk/discover/what-do-
wasps-do.html>.

12 World Health Organization, 'Onchocerciasis'.

13 See Sharon Dirckx, *Am I Just My Brain?* (Epsom: The Good Book Company, 2019).

8 Why would God allow pandemics?

1 Katherine J. Wu, 'There Are More Viruses Than Stars in the Universe. Why Do Only Some Infect Us?', *National Geographic*, 15 April 2020, <https://www.nationalgeographic.com/science/2020/04/factors-allow-viruses-infect-humans-coronavirus/>.

2 Ibid.

3 'What If All Viruses Disappeared?', Global Health Institute, University of Wisconsin–Madison, 18 June 2020, <https://ghi.wisc.edu/what-if-all-viruses-disappeared/>.

4 David Quammen, 'How Viruses Shape Our World', *National Geographic*, February 2021, <https://www.nationalgeographic.com/magazine/article/viruses-can-cause-great-harm-but-we-could-not-live-without-them-feature>.

5 Job 1:1.

6 Job 42:7.

7 Job 1:7b.

8 Matt. 4:23.

9 Luke 4:18–19.

9 Why doesn't God just intervene anyway?

1 *Alpha* course, <https://alpha.org>.

2 'Alpha Film Series Episode 15: Does God Heal Today', YouTube, 31 May 2020, <https://www.youtube.com/watch?v=jZH8M_zj5XY>.

3 Tom Holland, *Dominion* (London: Abacus, 2020), p. 25.

4 For example, Matt. 22:37–39.

5 Holland, *Dominion*, p. 123.

6 Rodney Stark, *The Rise of Christianity* (New York: HarperCollins, 1996), p. 76.

7 Ps. 22:1–2, 14–15.

8 Ps. 23:1–4.

9 Isa. 53:3a.

10 Col. 2:15.

11 Isa. 53:5.

12 Rom. 5:3b–5.

13 2 Cor. 1:3–4.

14 Rev. 21:3b–4.

15 For example, Gary R. Habermas and Michael R. Licona, *The Case for the Resurrection of Jesus* (Grand Rapids, MI: Kregel, 2004); Lee Strobel, *The Case for Christ* (Grand Rapids, MI: Zondervan, 1998).

16 1 Cor. 15:42–44.

17 2 Pet. 3:9.

10 What should my response be to a natural disaster?

1 Erik Stokstad, 'When COVID-19 Silenced Cities, Birdsong Recaptured Its Former Glory', *Science*, 24 September 2020, <https://www.sciencemag.org/news/2020/09/when-covid-19-silenced-cities-birdsong-recaptured-its-former-glory>.

2 'Royal Society for the Prevention of Cruelty to Animals', Wikipedia, last updated 14 September 2022, <https://en.wikipedia.org/wiki/Royal_Society_for_the_Prevention_of_Cruelty_to_Animals>.

3 Gen. 1:28.

4 Matt. 7:12.

5 'Effective Altruism Global', Effective Altruism, <https://www.eamanchester.org/about>.

6 Robin Levinson-King, 'Faith and Spirituality in the Time of Covid', BBC News online, <https://www.bbc.co.uk/news/world-us-canada-55419894>.

7 *Alpha*, <https://alpha.org>.

8 *Christianity Explored*, <https://www.christianityexplored.org>.

9 For starters, check out Simon Edwards, *The Sanity of Belief: Why Faith Makes Sense* (London: SPCK, 2021) and the Oxford Centre for Christian Apologetics, <www.theocca.org>.

10 John 11:25–26.

11 Sydney Page, 'Italian Couple "Romeo and Juliet" Met from Their Balconies During Lockdown. Now They're Engaged', *Washington Post*, 24 September 2020, <https://www.washingtonpost.com/lifestyle/2020/09/24/italian-couple-romeo-juliet-met-their-balconies-during-lockdown-now-theyre-engaged/>.